A Walk Near Boston

A Walk Near Boston is 44 photographs from a walk
in mostly Somerville and Cambridge MA
(and the flights there, and in the hotel)
during May 2025.

These images previously appeared in
a different form on my Instagram.

Published by Imaginary Dynamics
imaginarydynamics.com
ISBN: 978-1-971080-05-5

First Edition
File version 1 3 Z 342

There are no disclaimers, warranties, safety notices,
captions, or guarantees for this book or for anything in life.

A Walk Near Boston

Otto Kitsinger

A walk in mostly Somerville and Cambridge
(and the flights there, and in the hotel)
during May 2025.

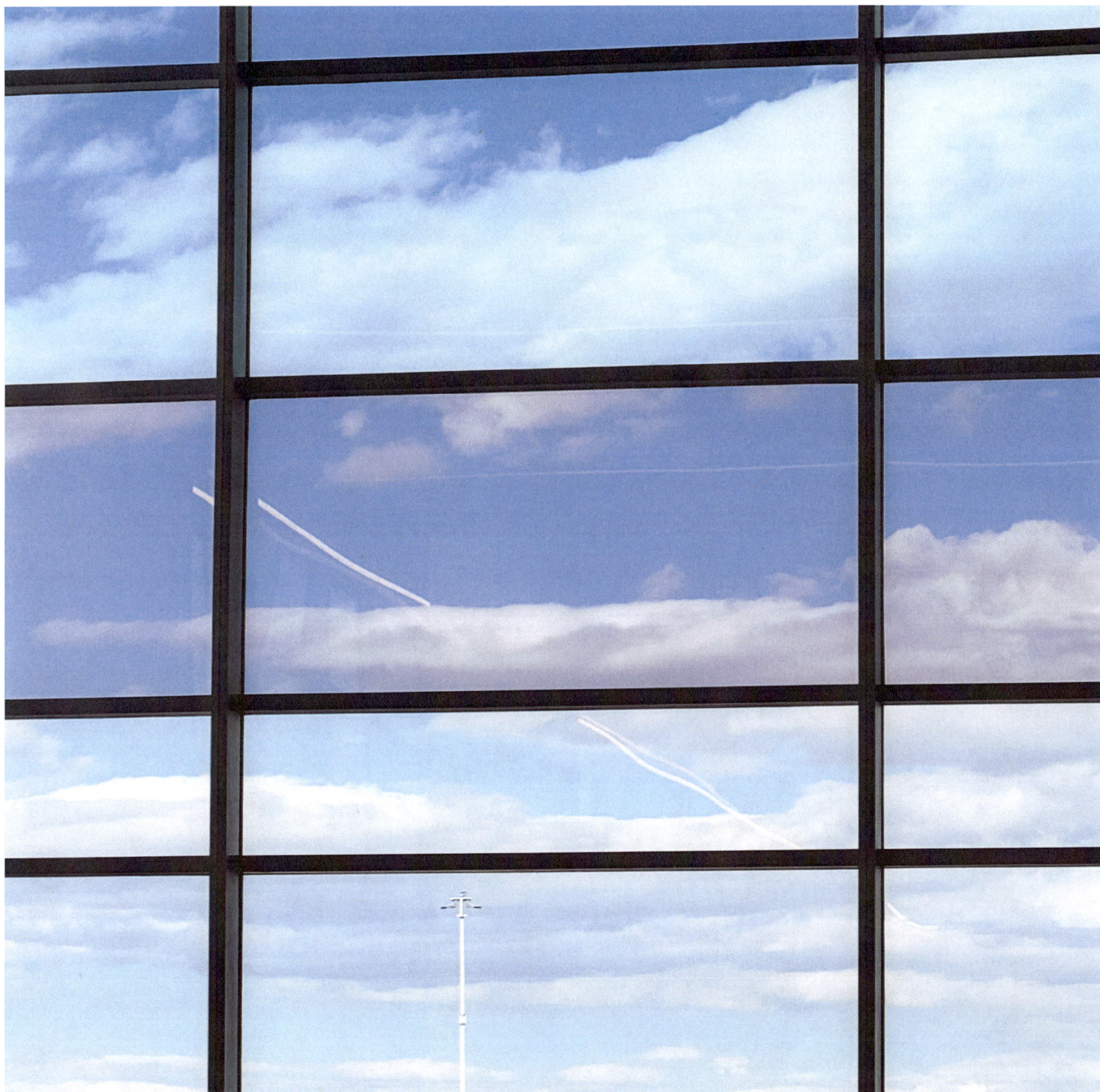

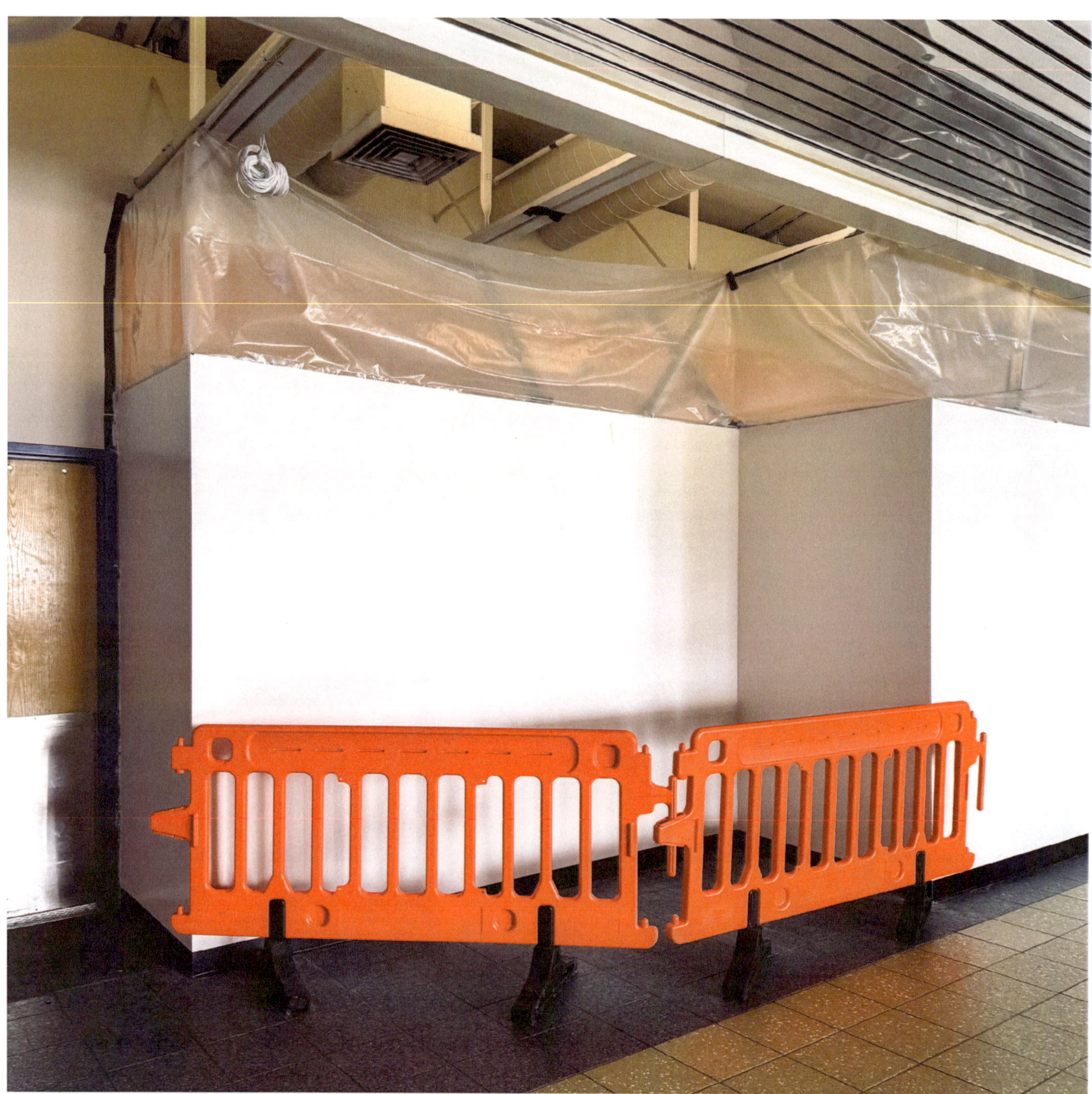

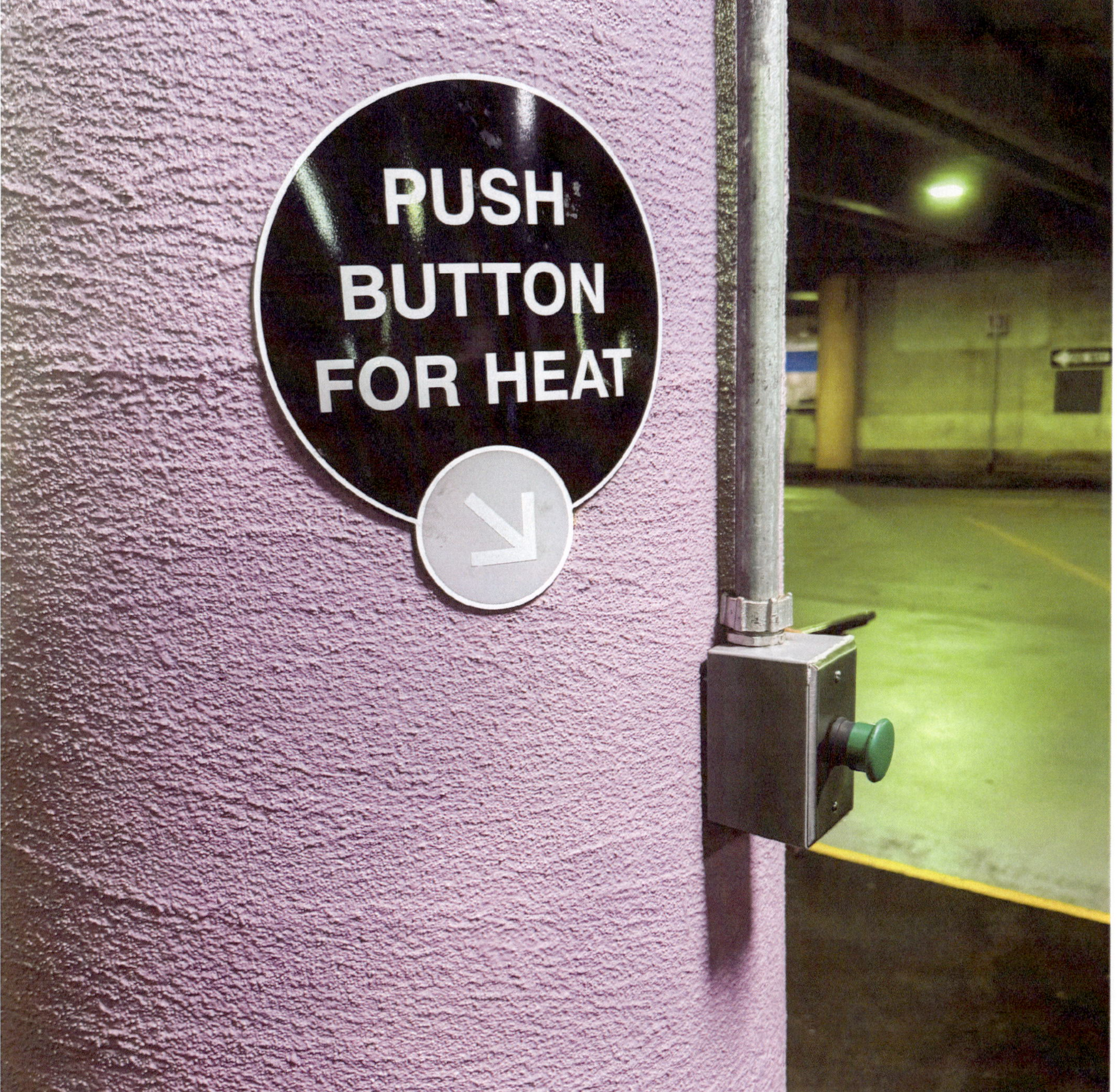
PUSH
BUTTON
FOR HEAT

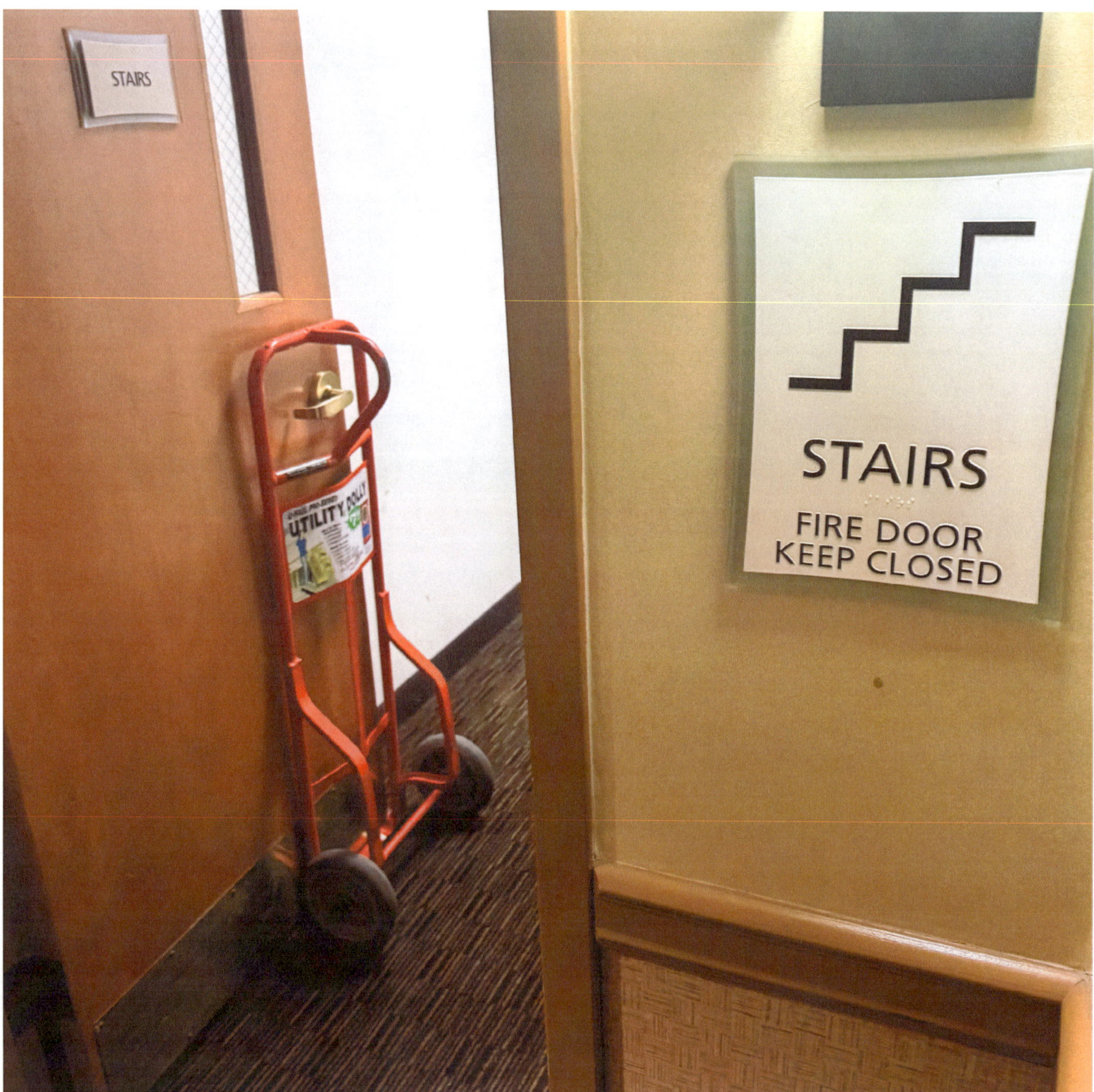
STAIRS
UTILITY DOLLY
STAIRS
FIRE DOOR
KEEP CLOSED

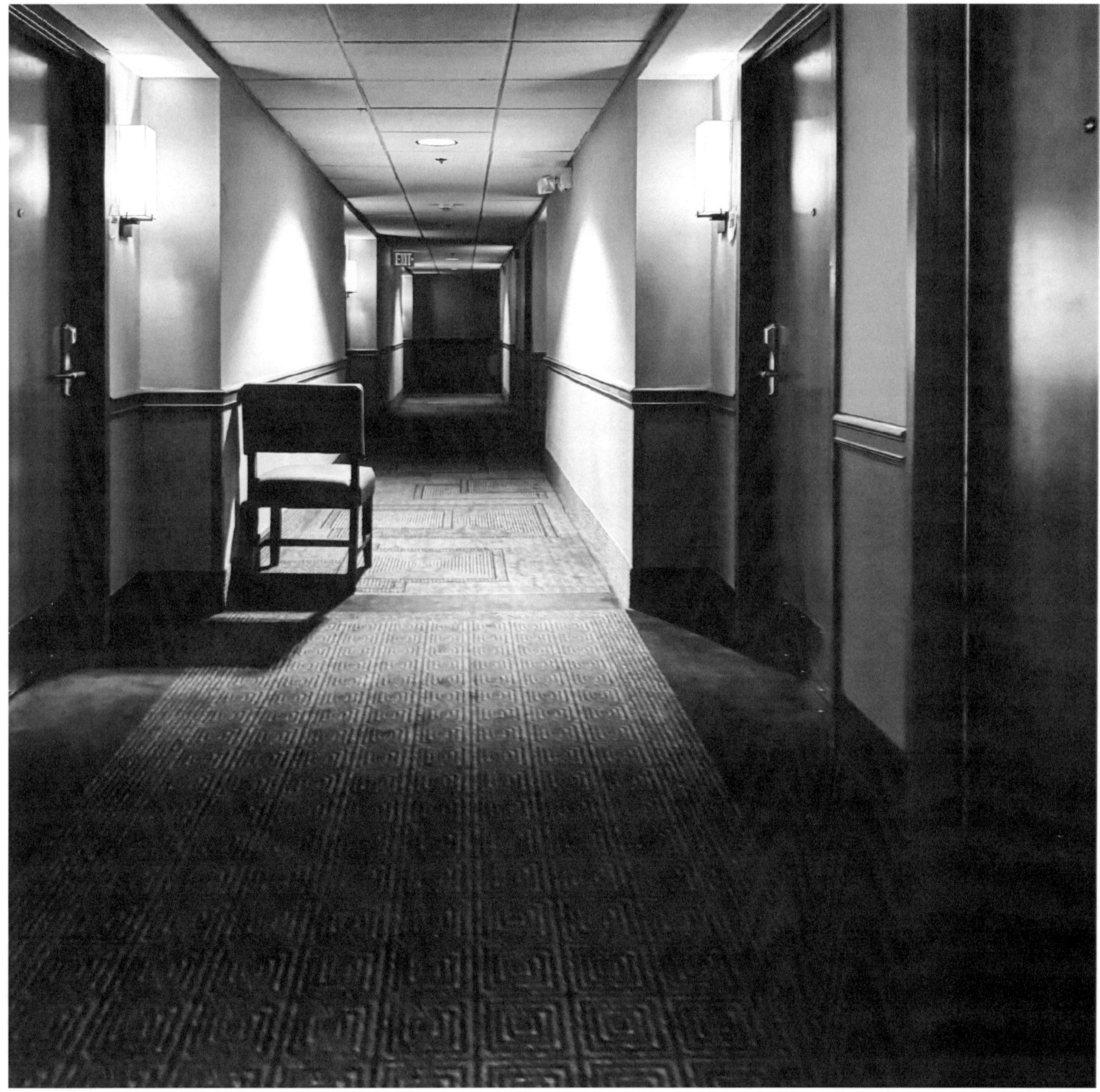

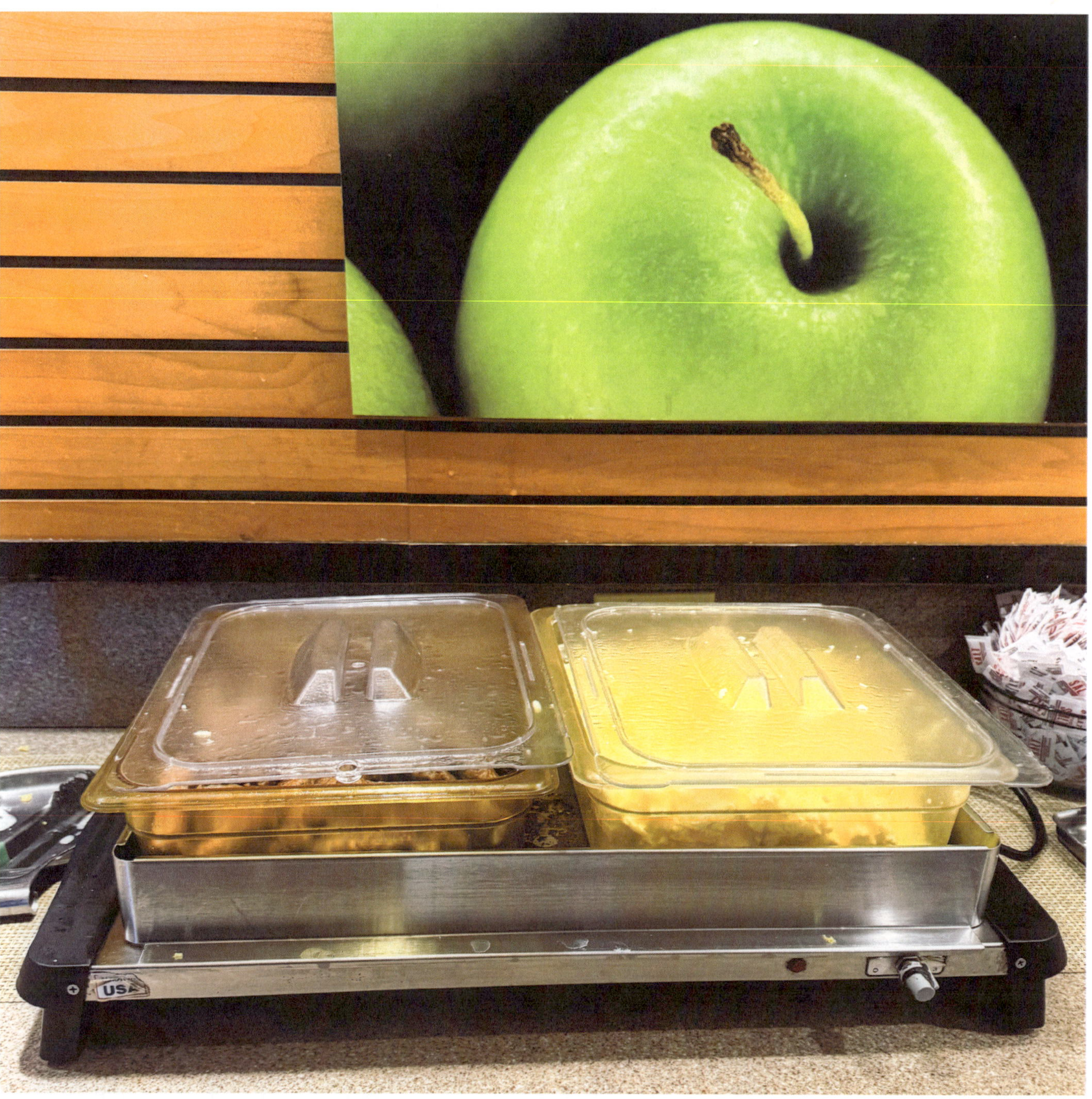

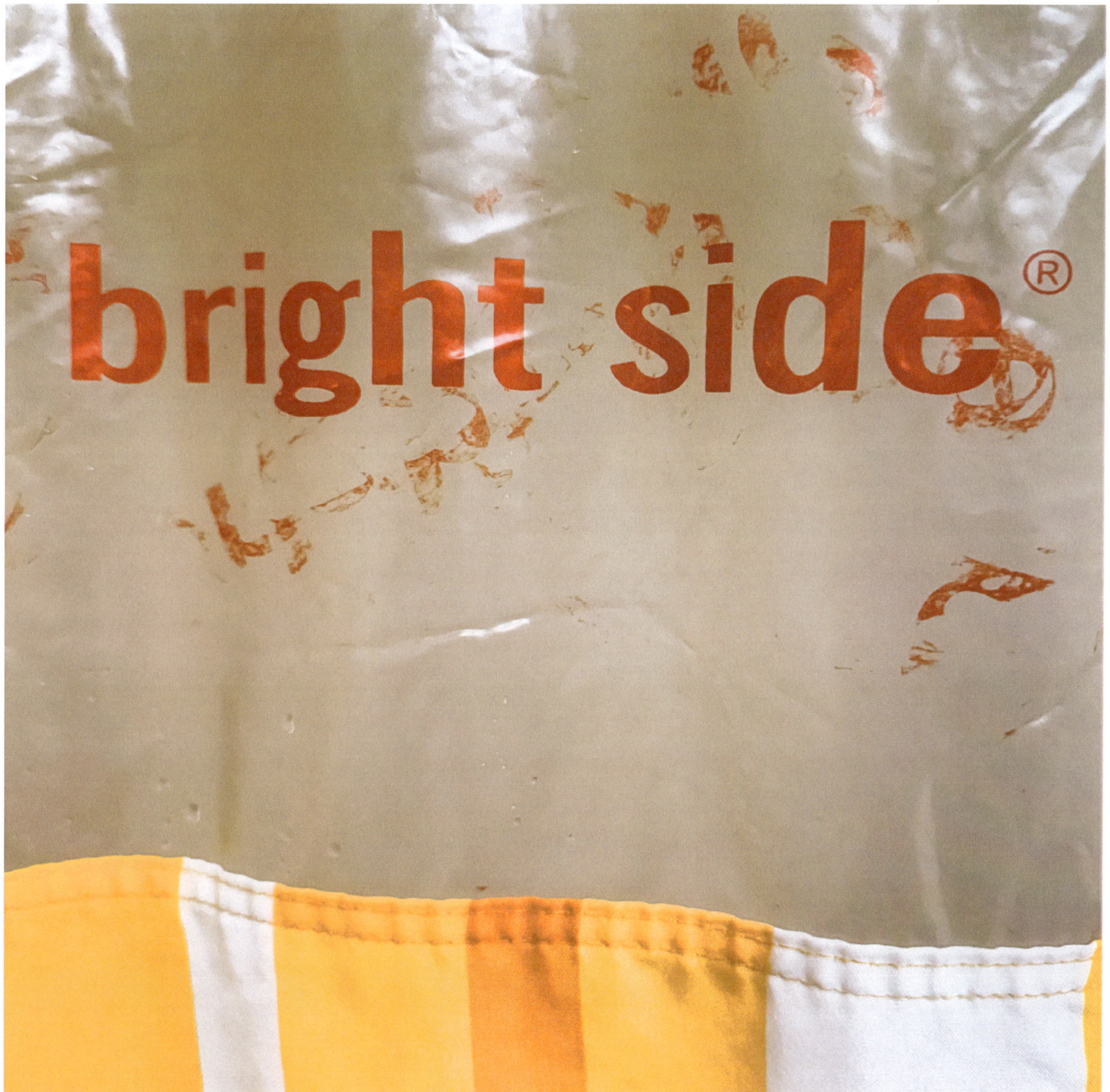

bright side®

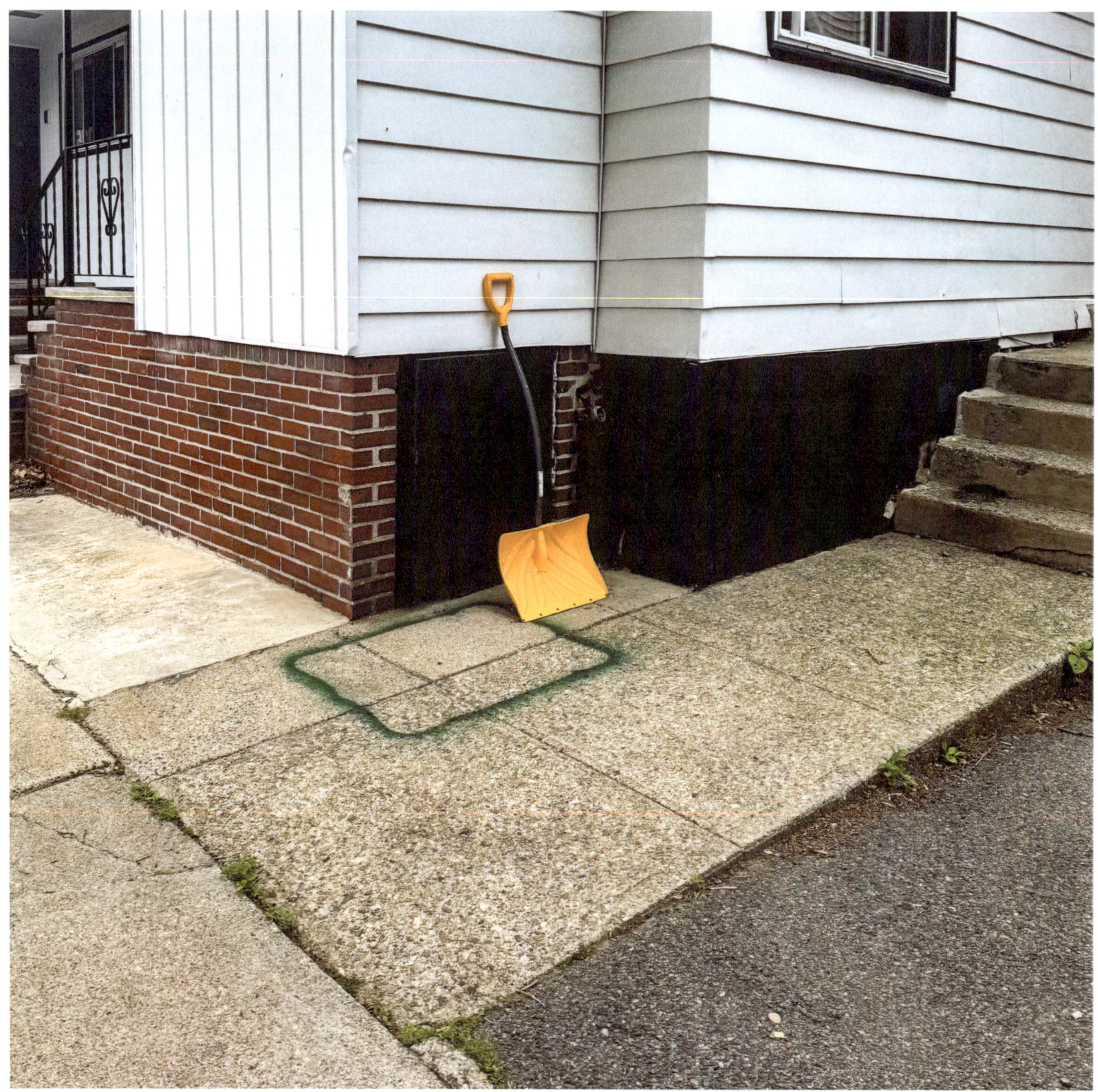

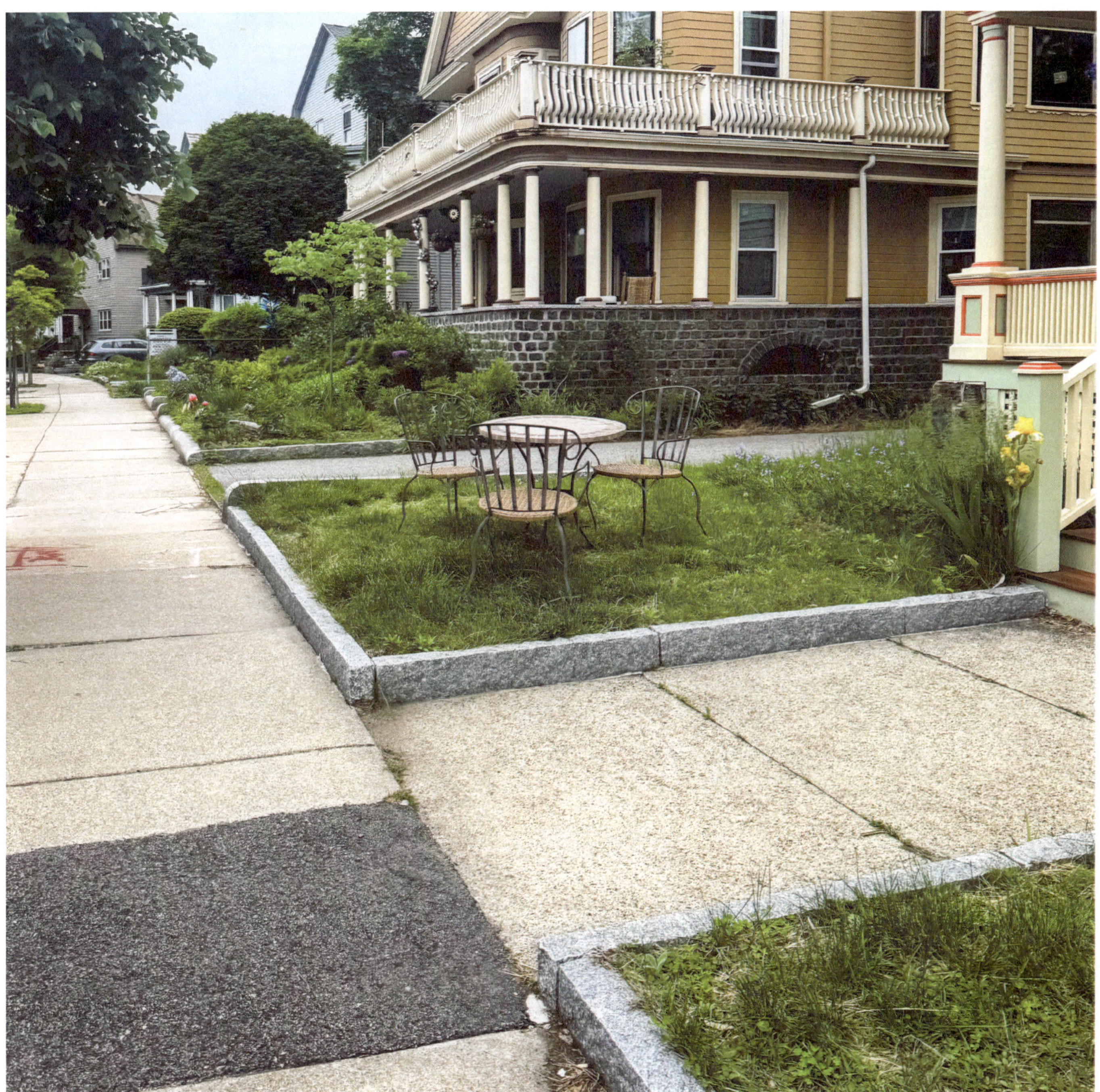

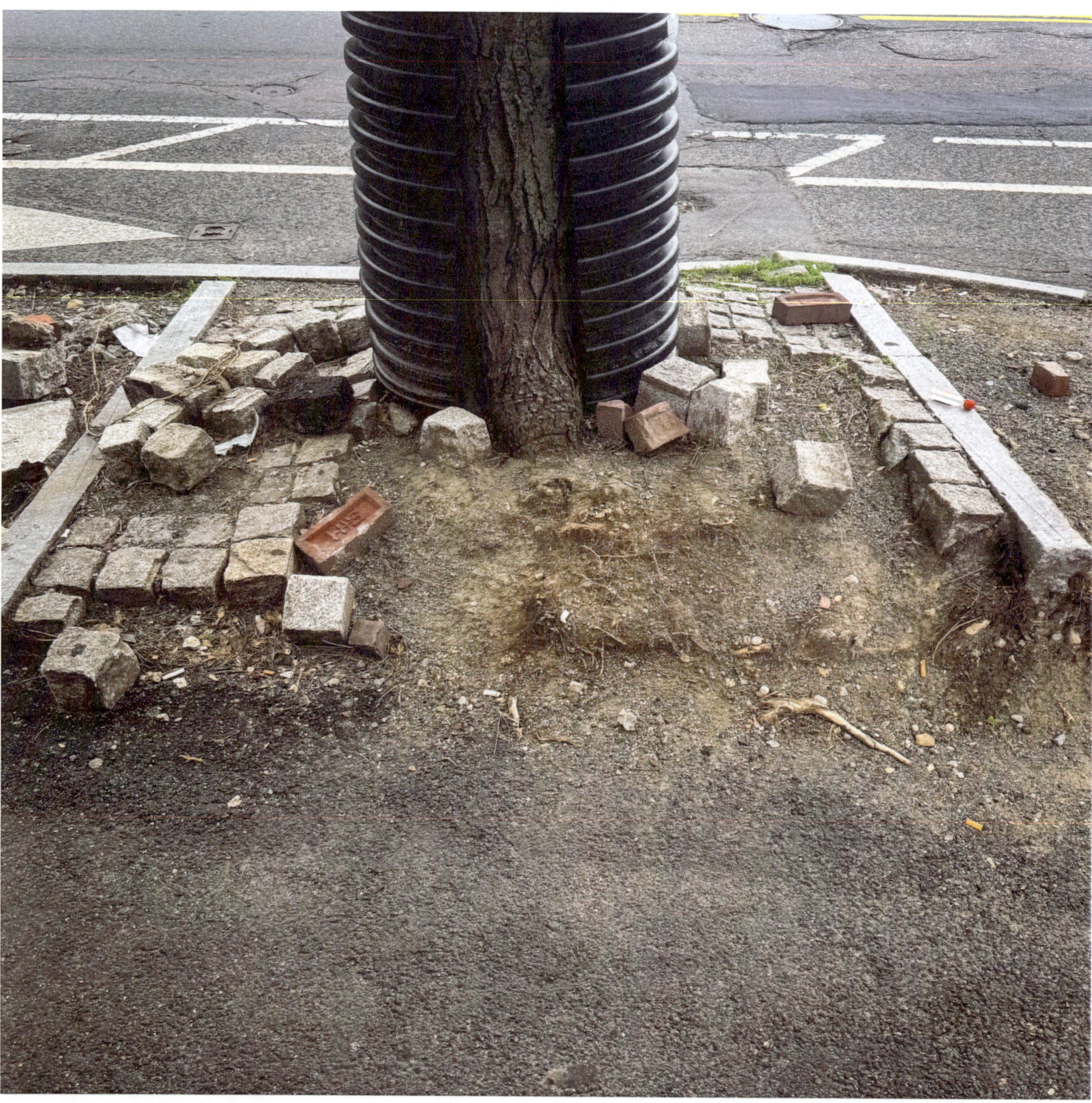

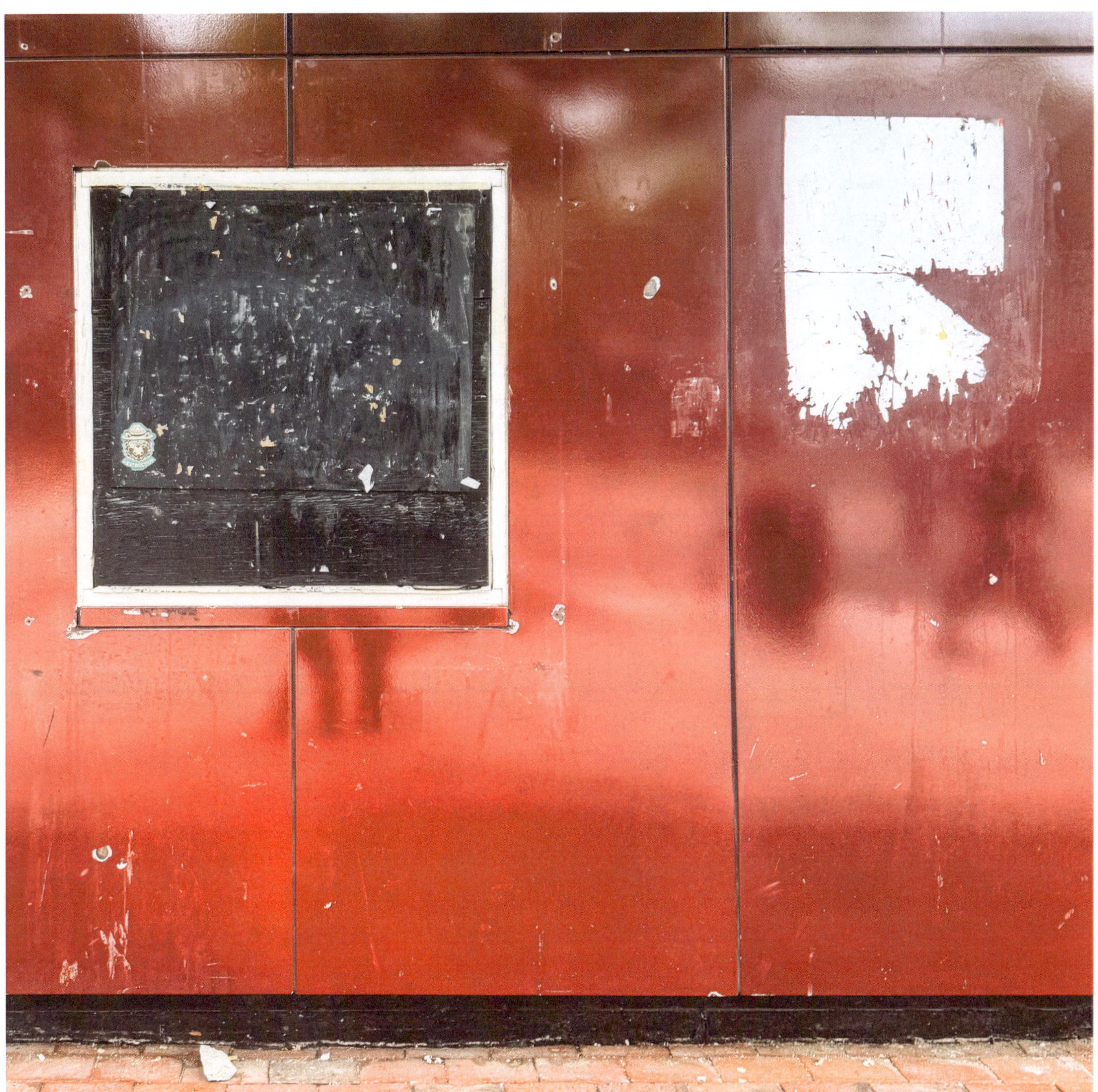

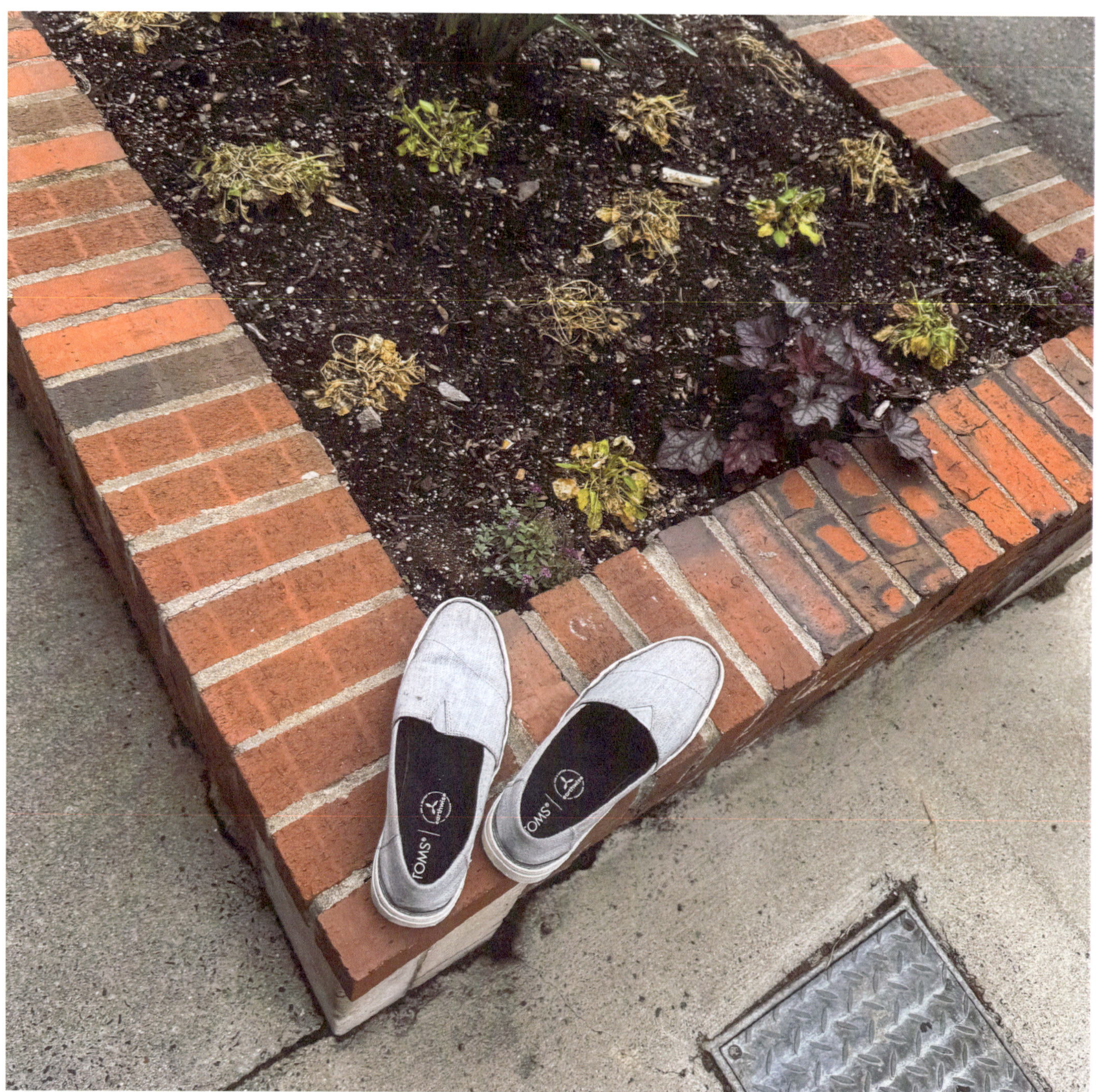

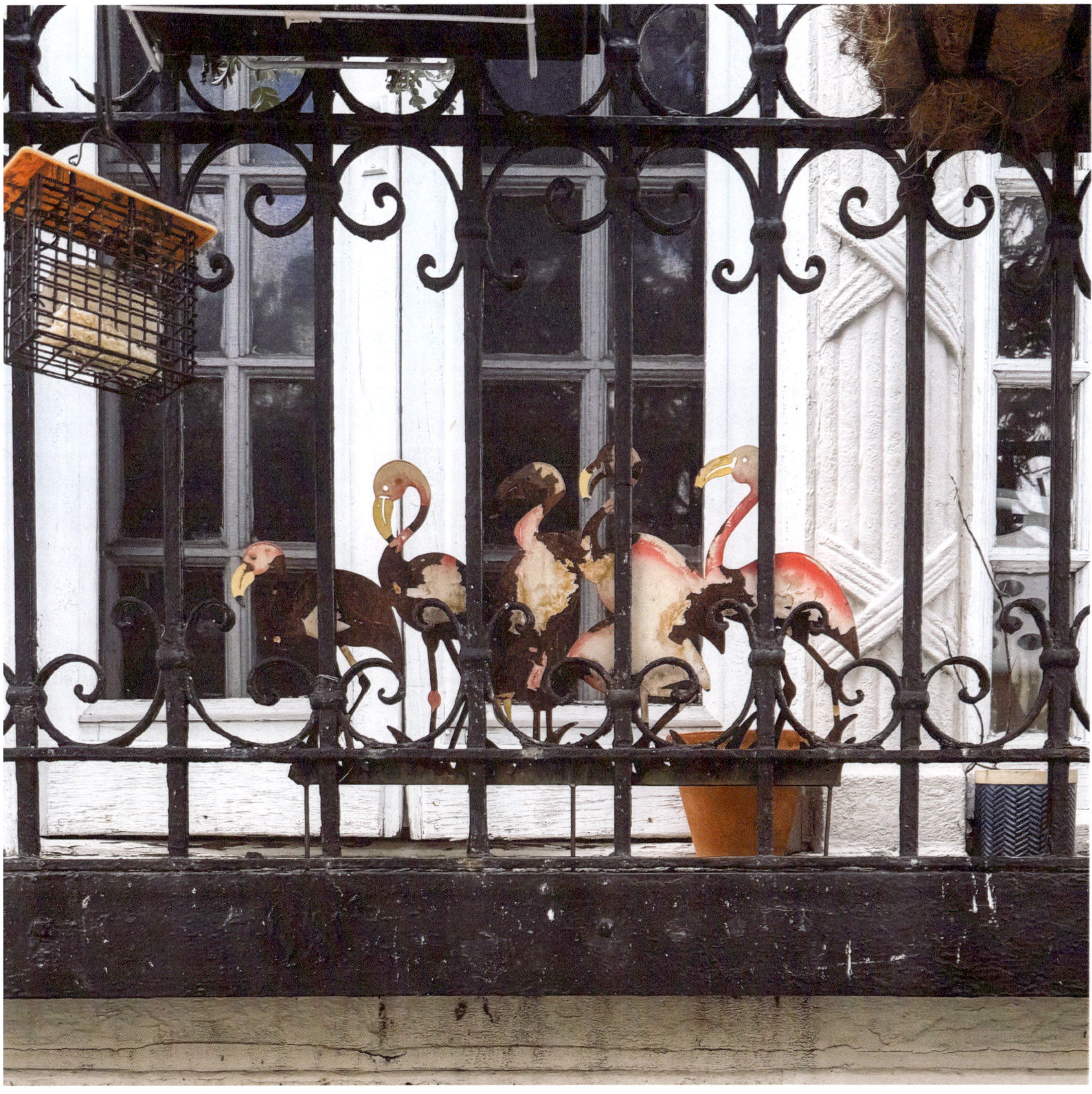

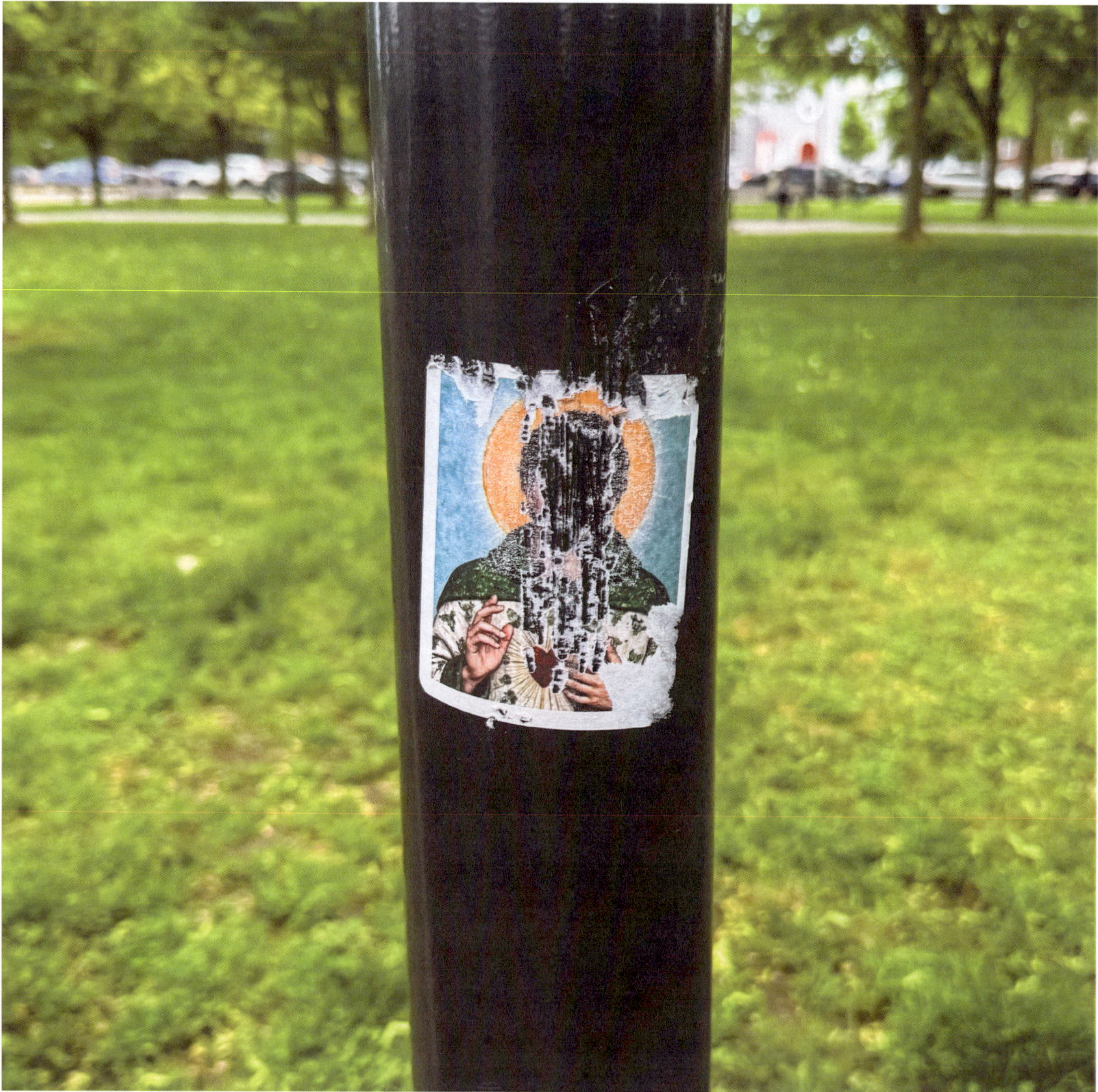

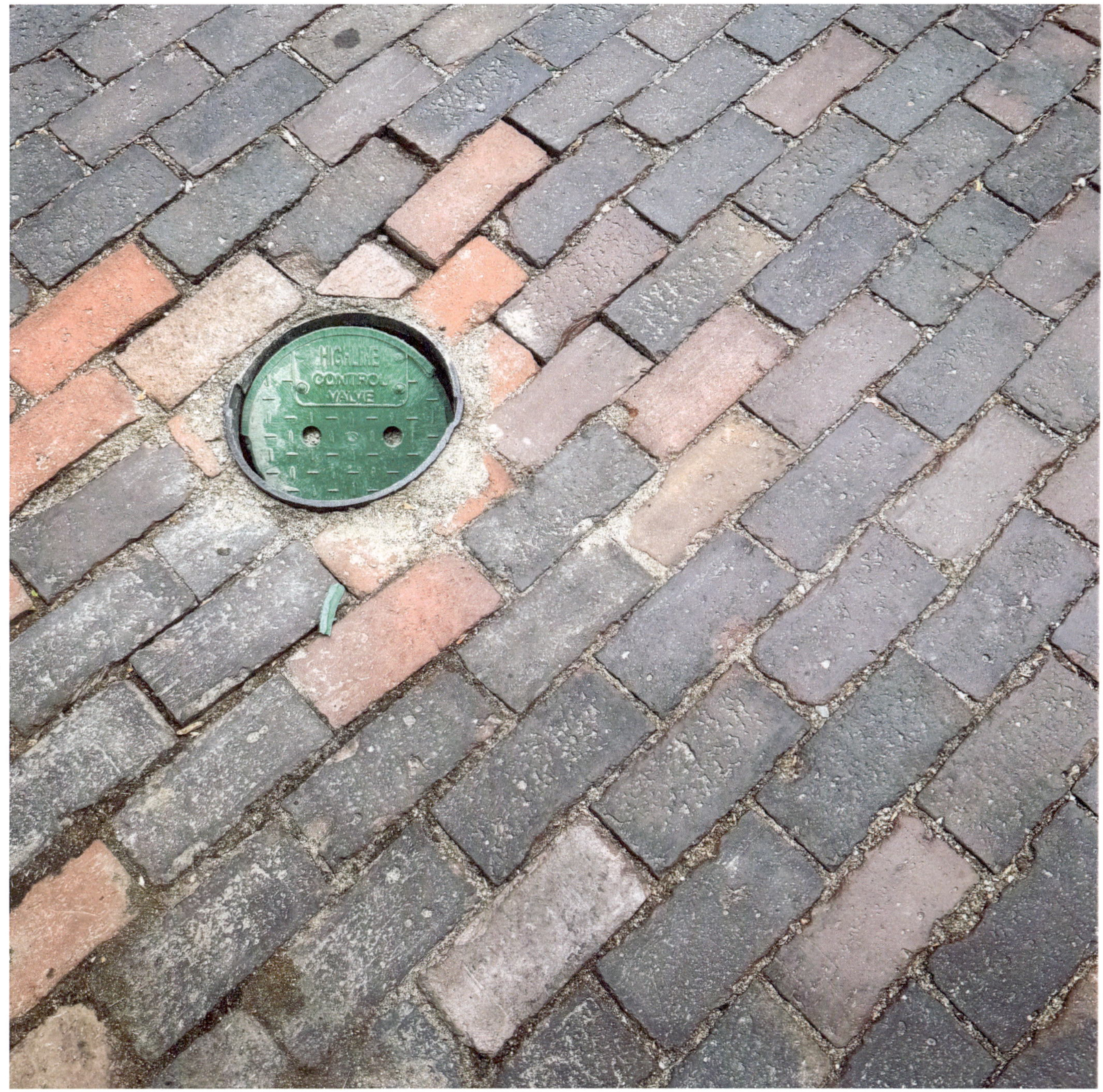

HIGHLINE
CONTROL
VALVE

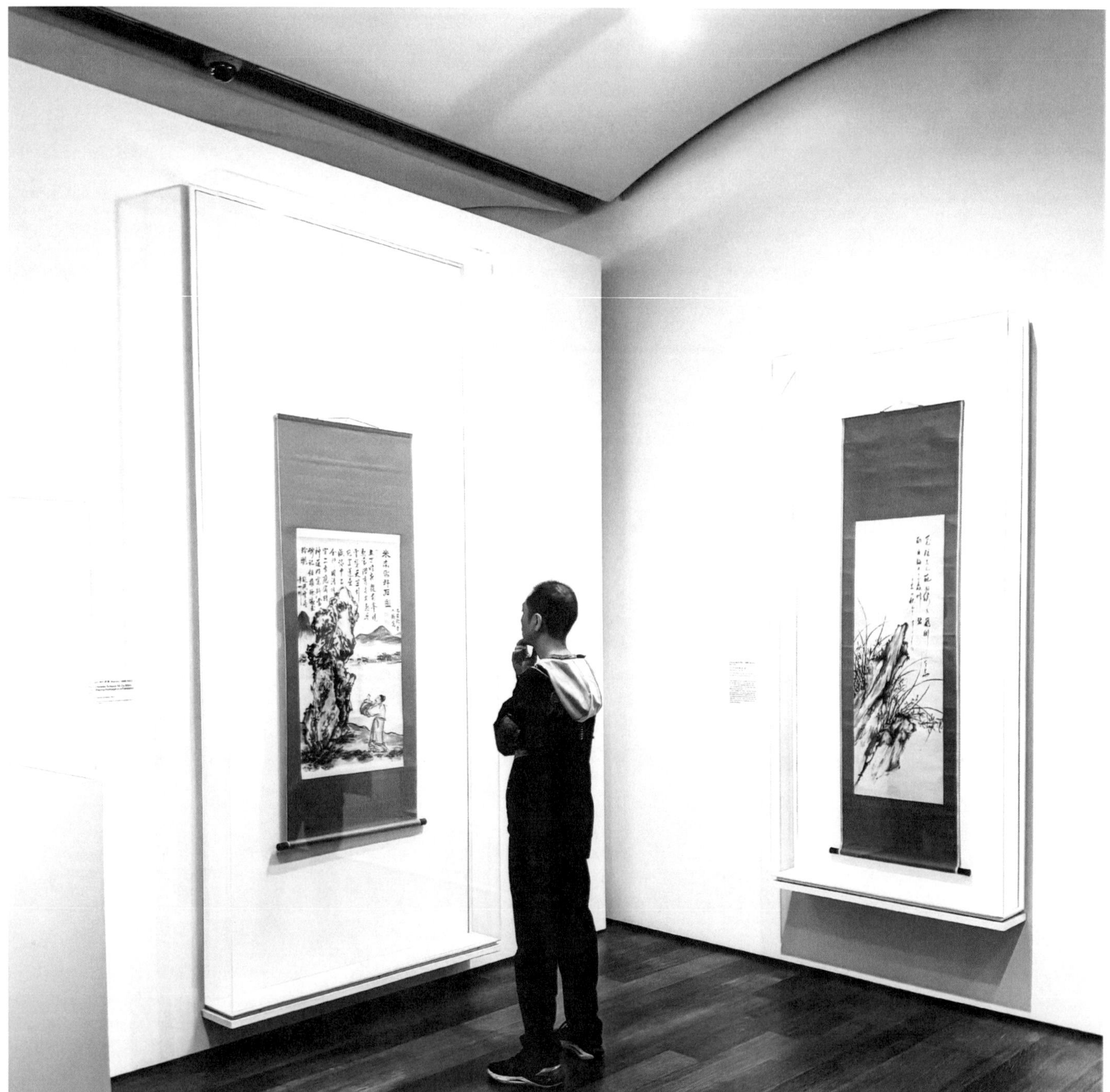

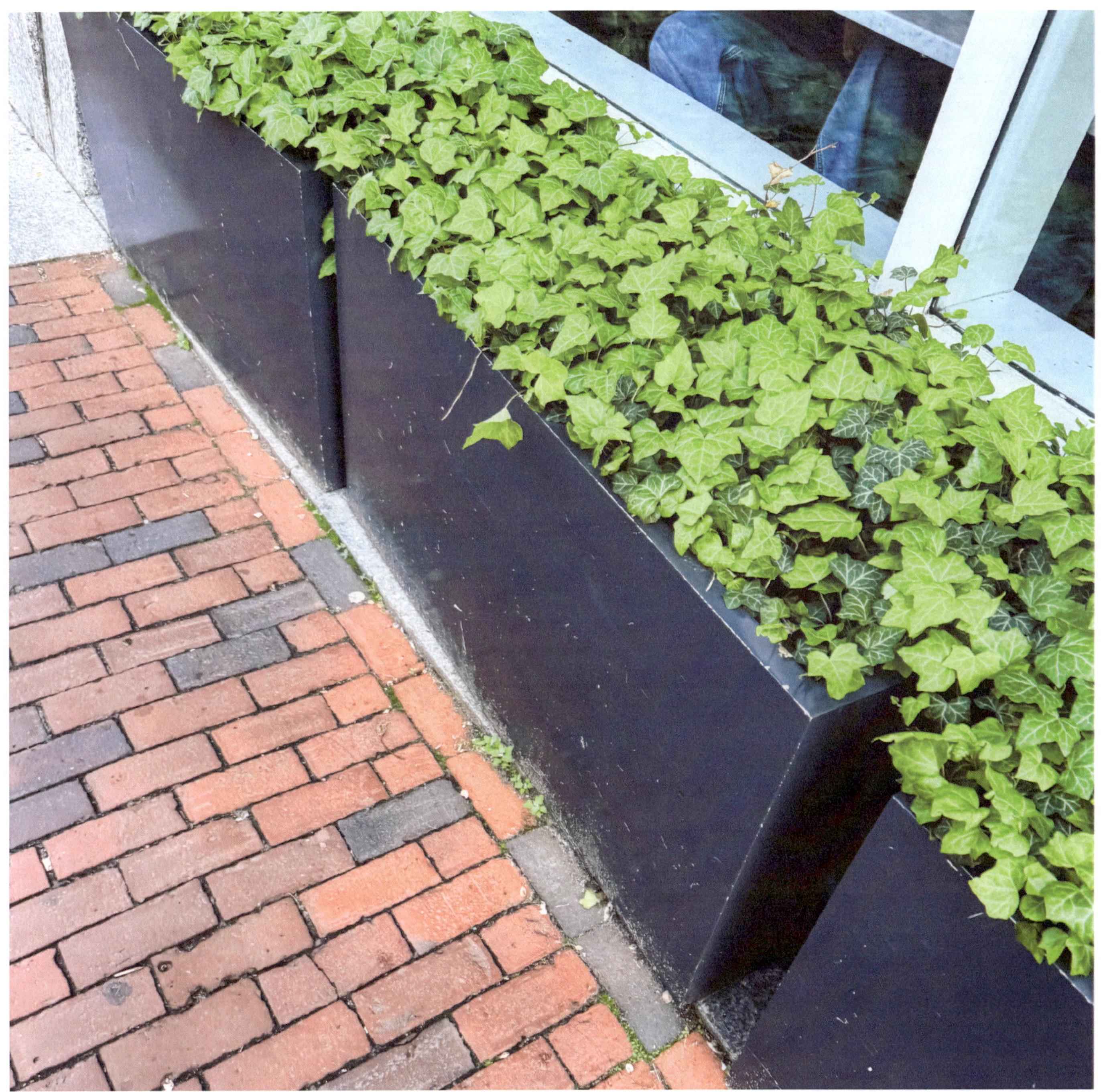

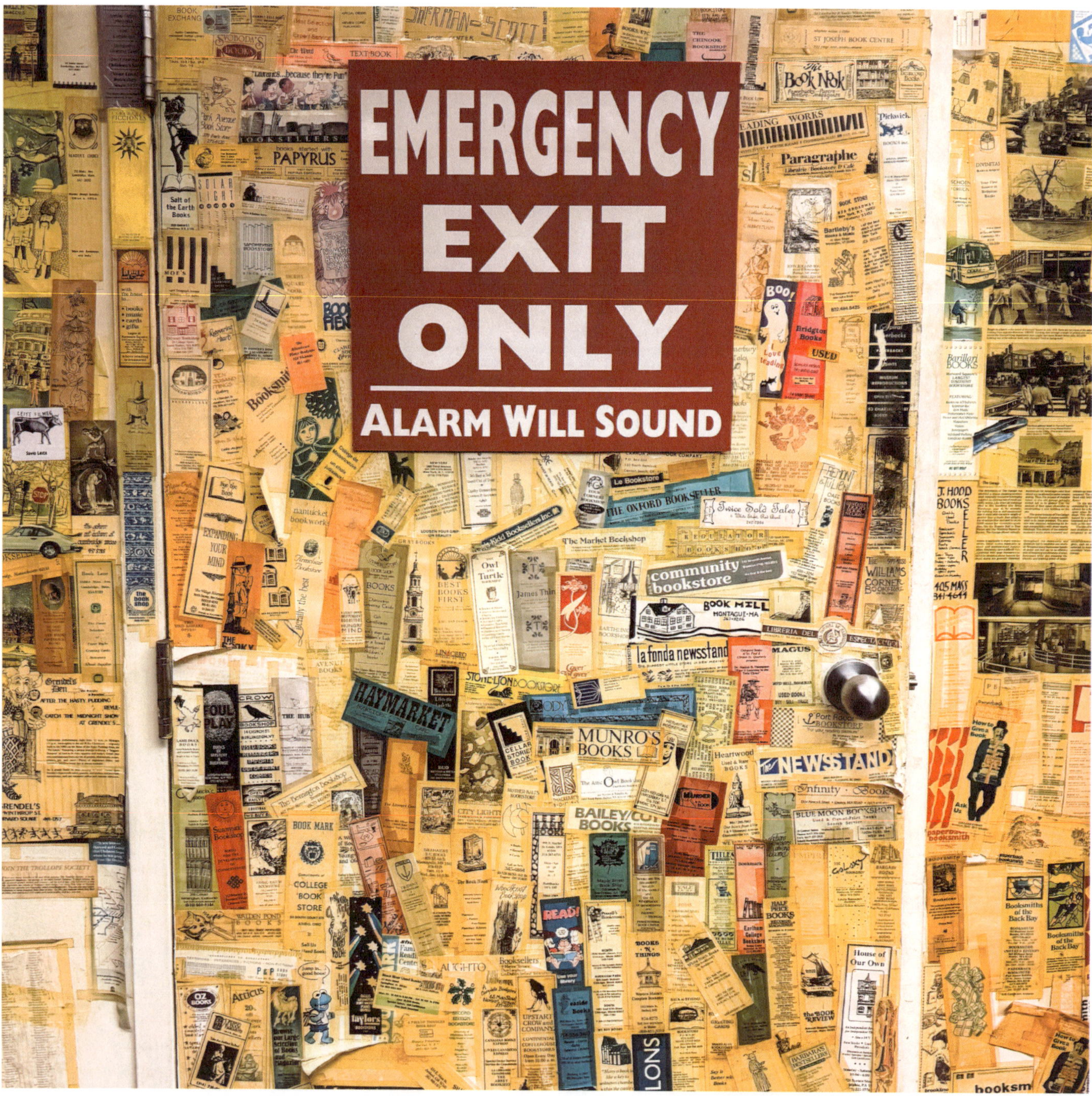
EMERGENCY
EXIT
ONLY
Alarm Will Sound

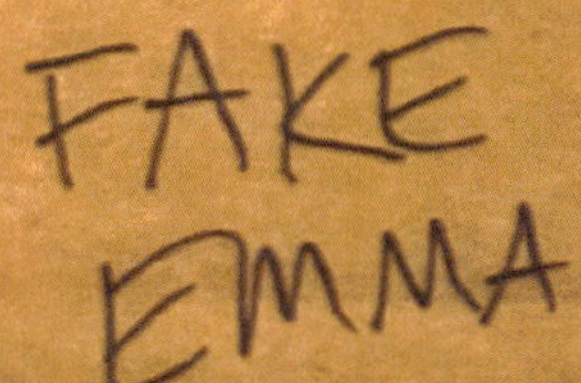

FAKE
EMMA
GREAT
JONES
BOOKS
GREAT
JONES

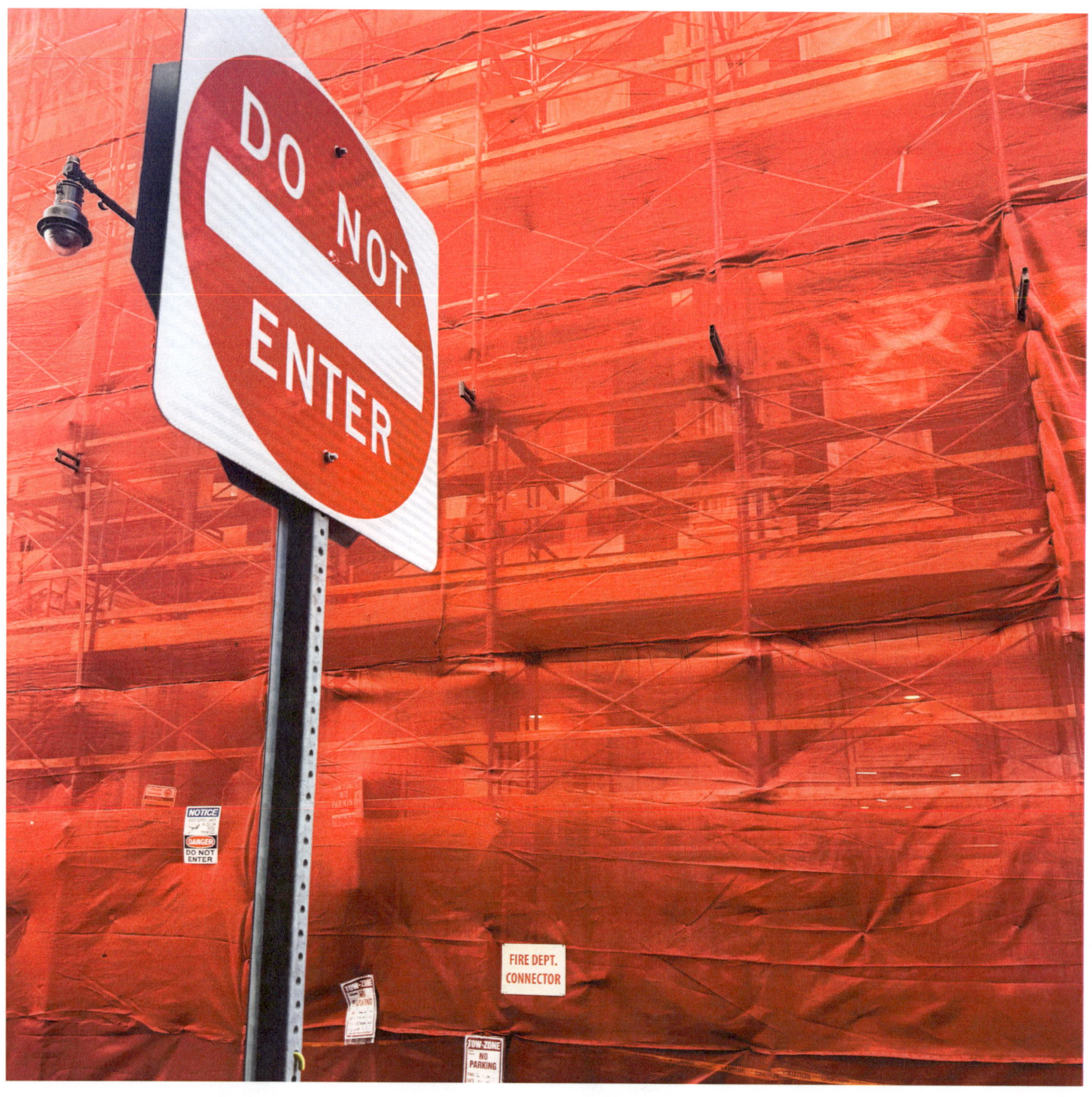

DO NOT
ENTER
FIRE DEPT.
CONNECTOR

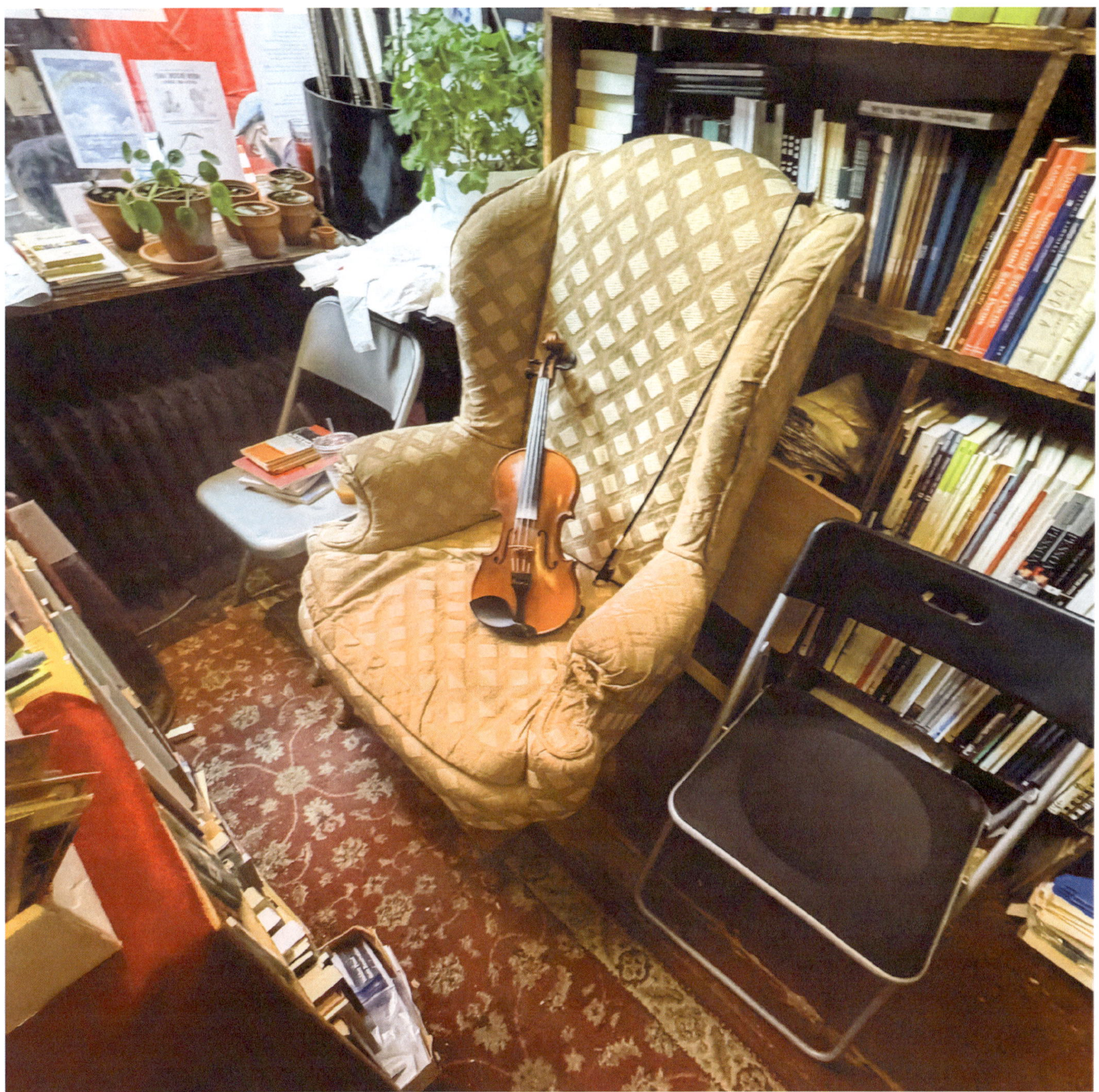

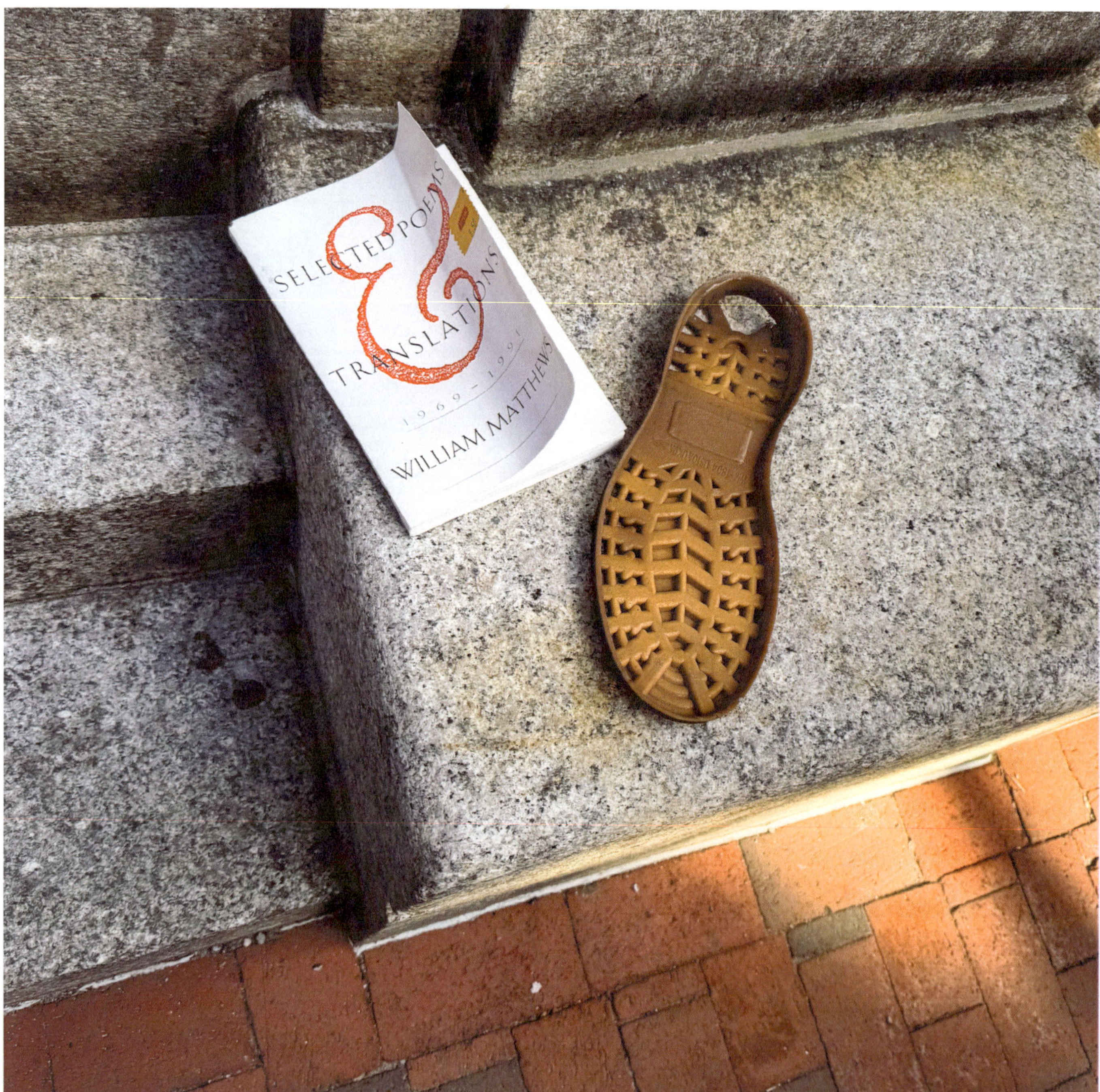

SELECTED POEMS
&
TRANSLATIONS
1969 - 1991
WILLIAM MATTHEWS

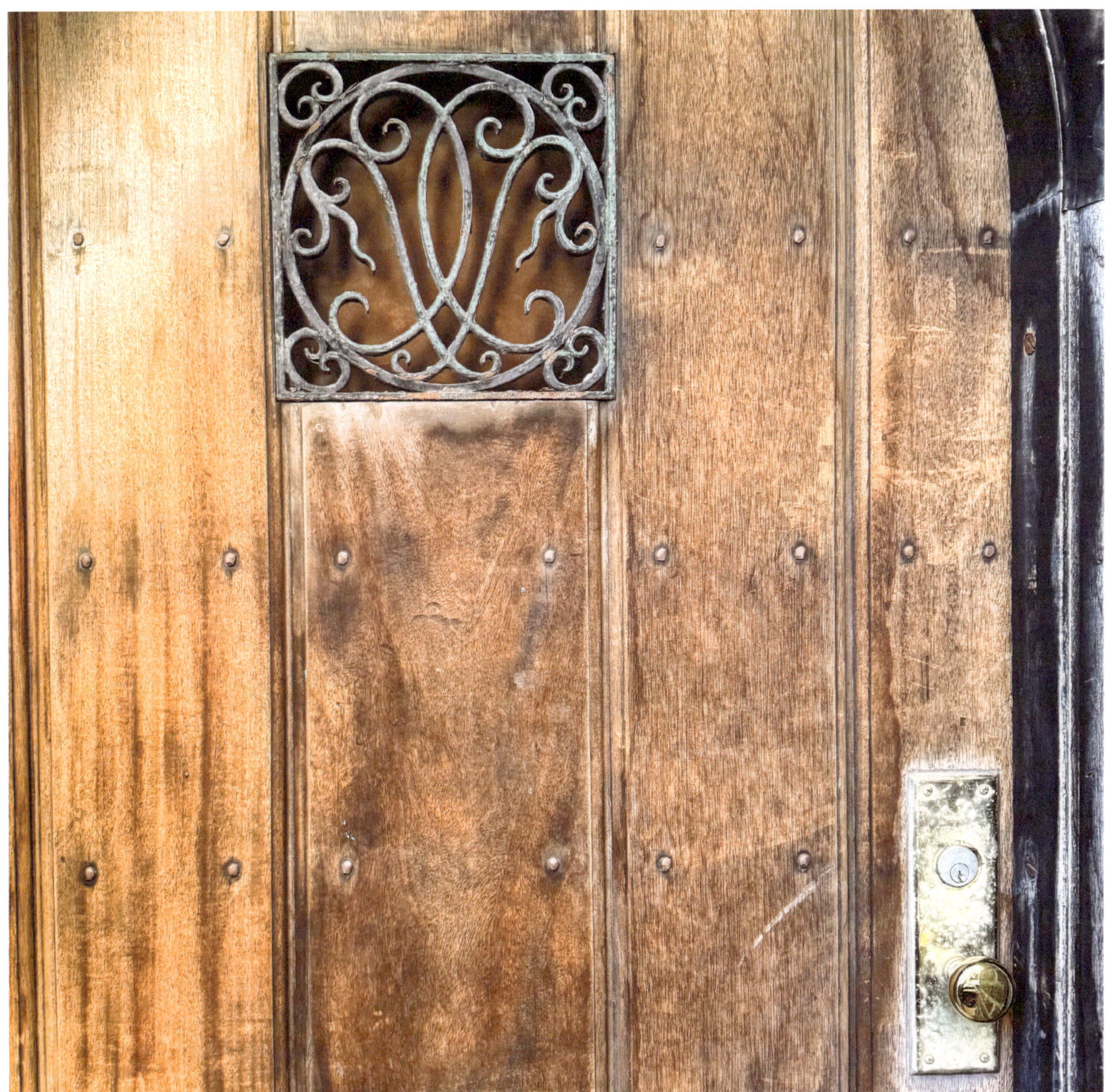

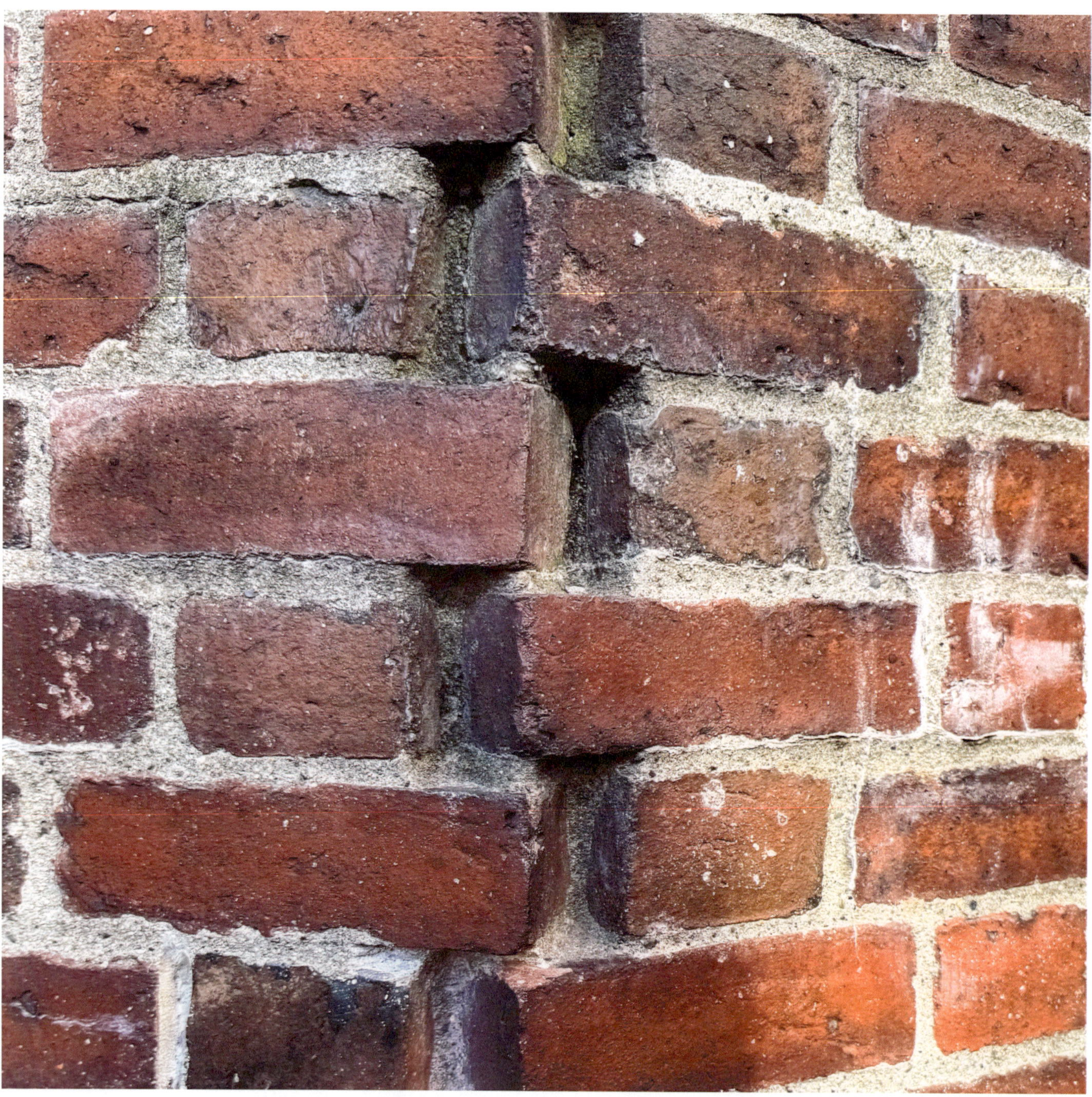

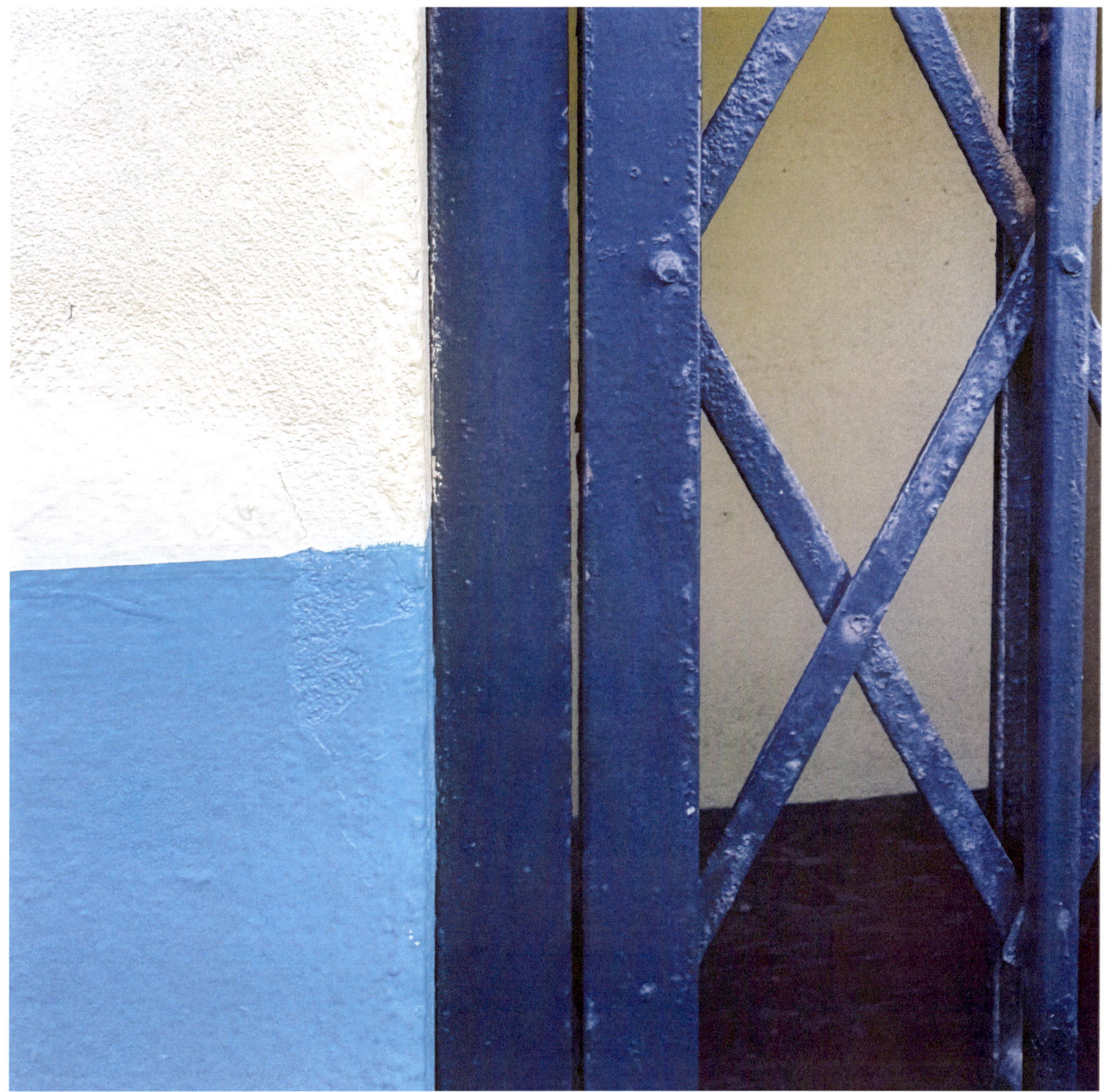

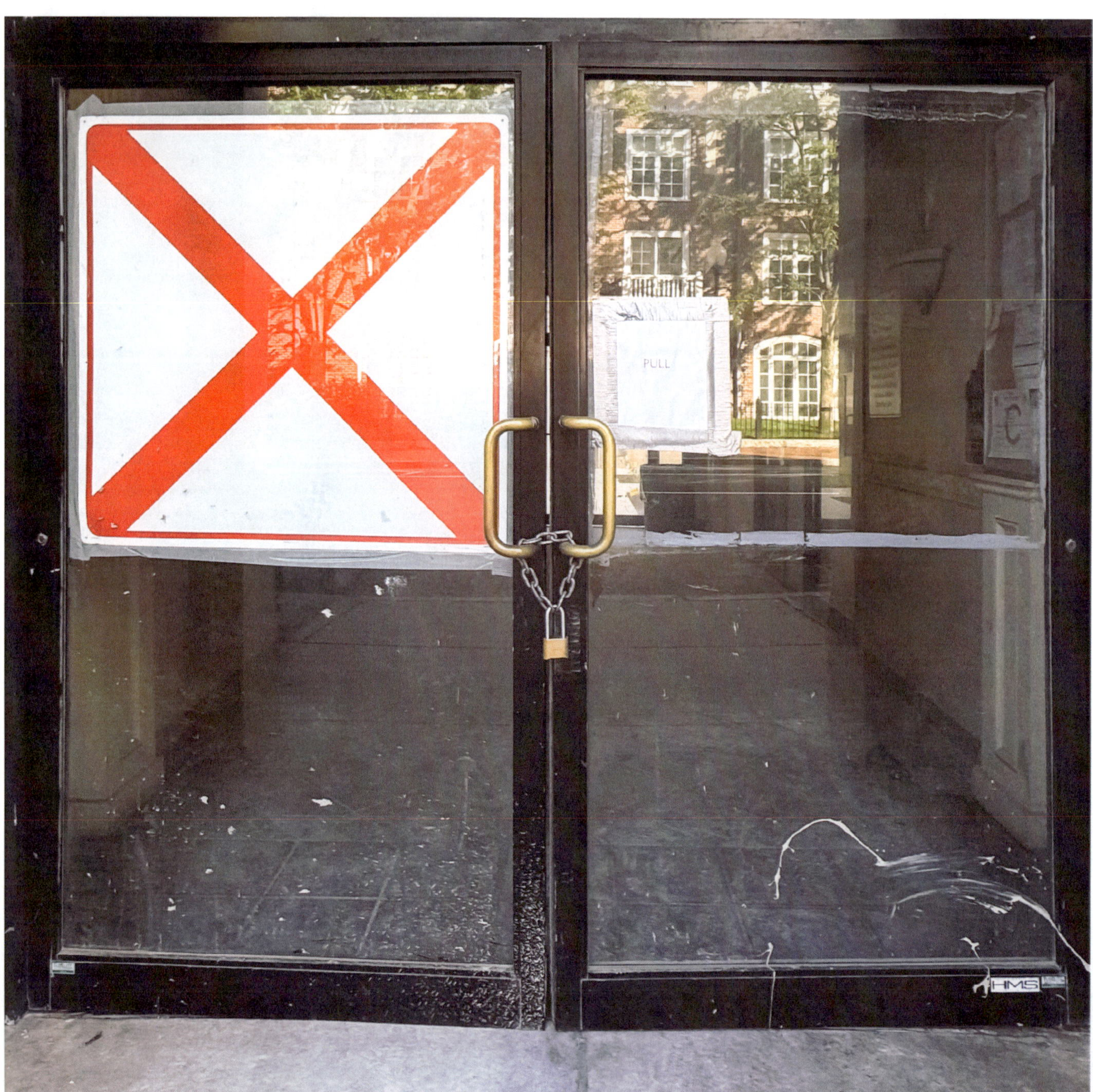

PULL
HMS

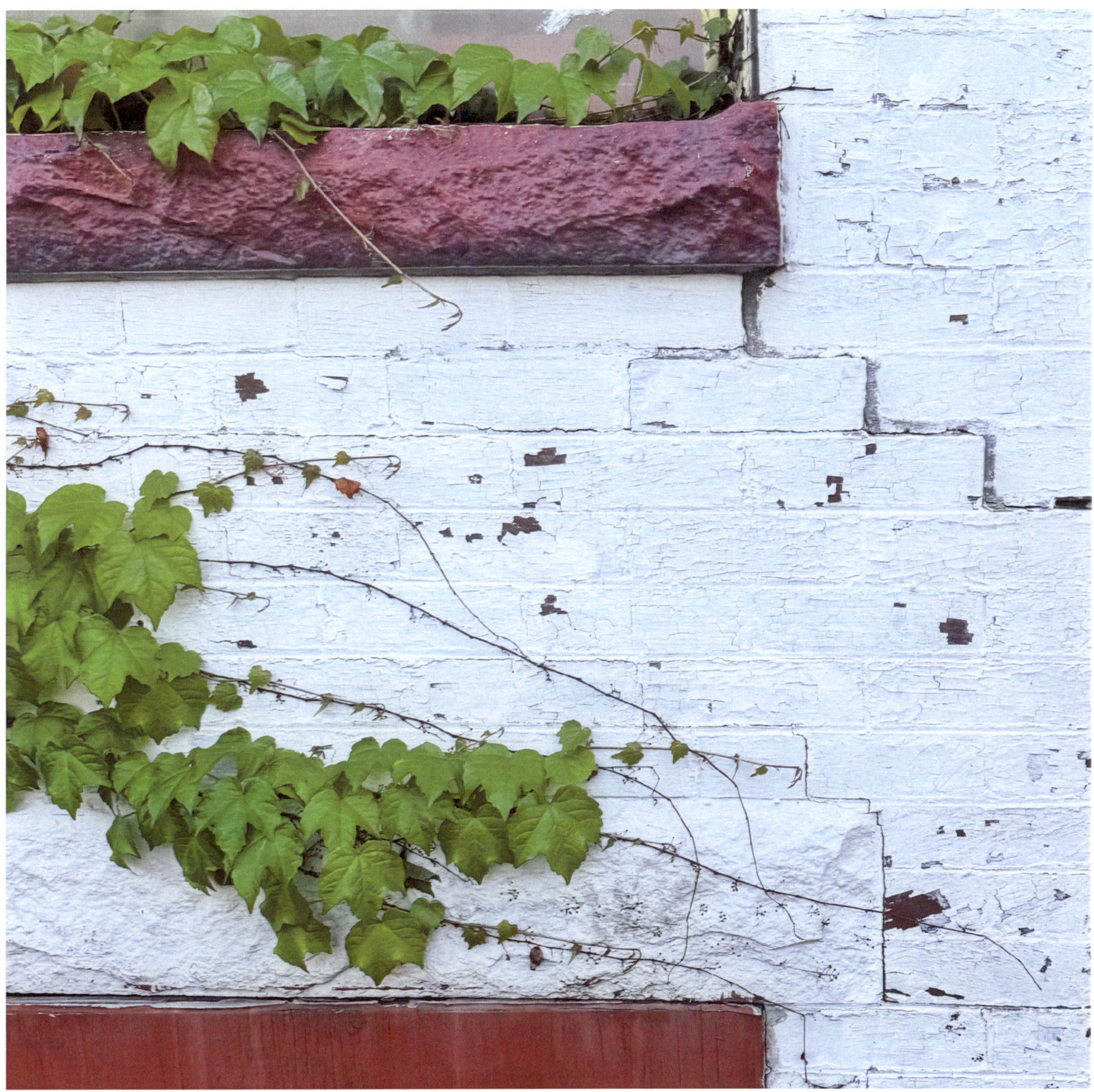

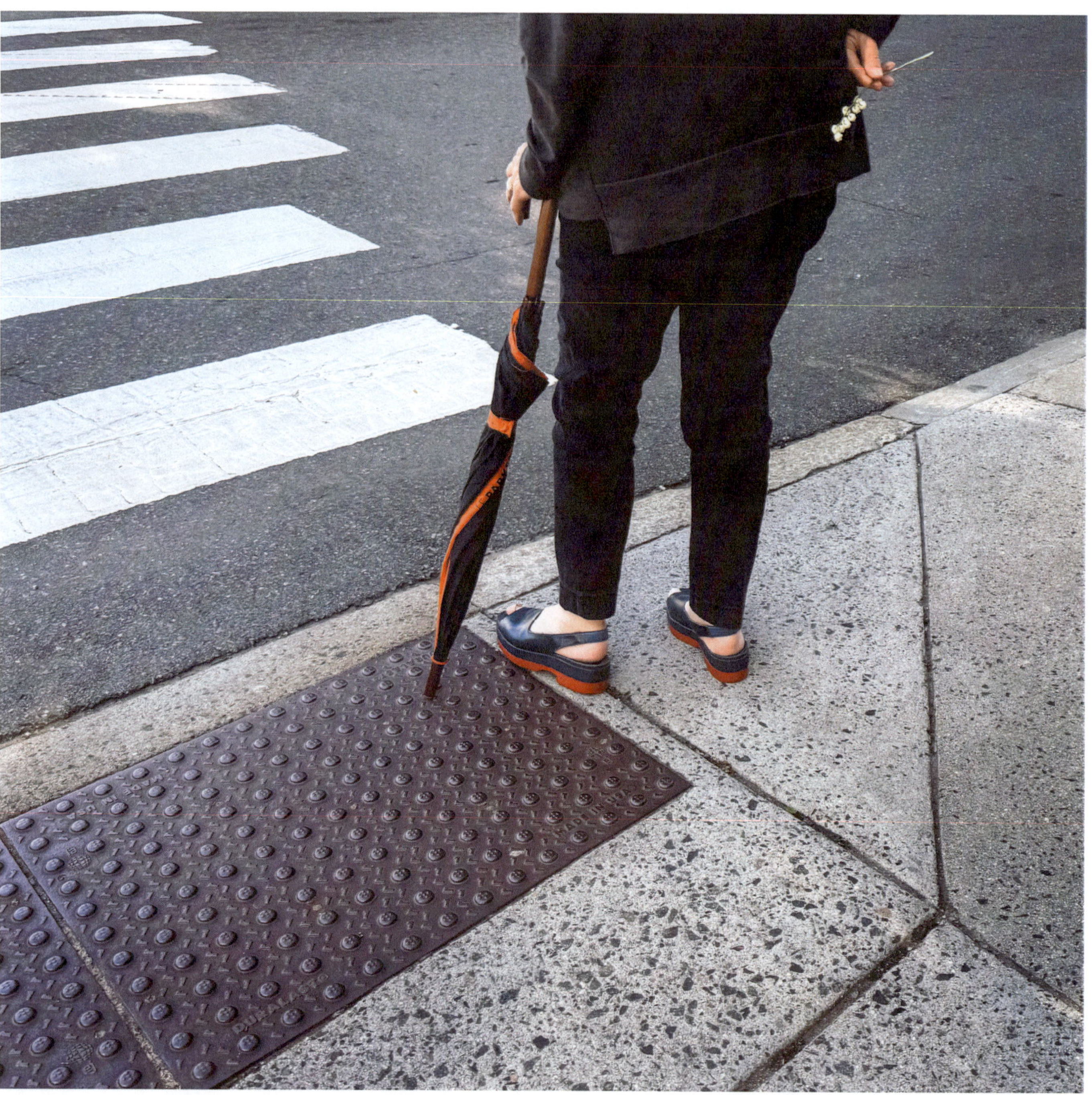

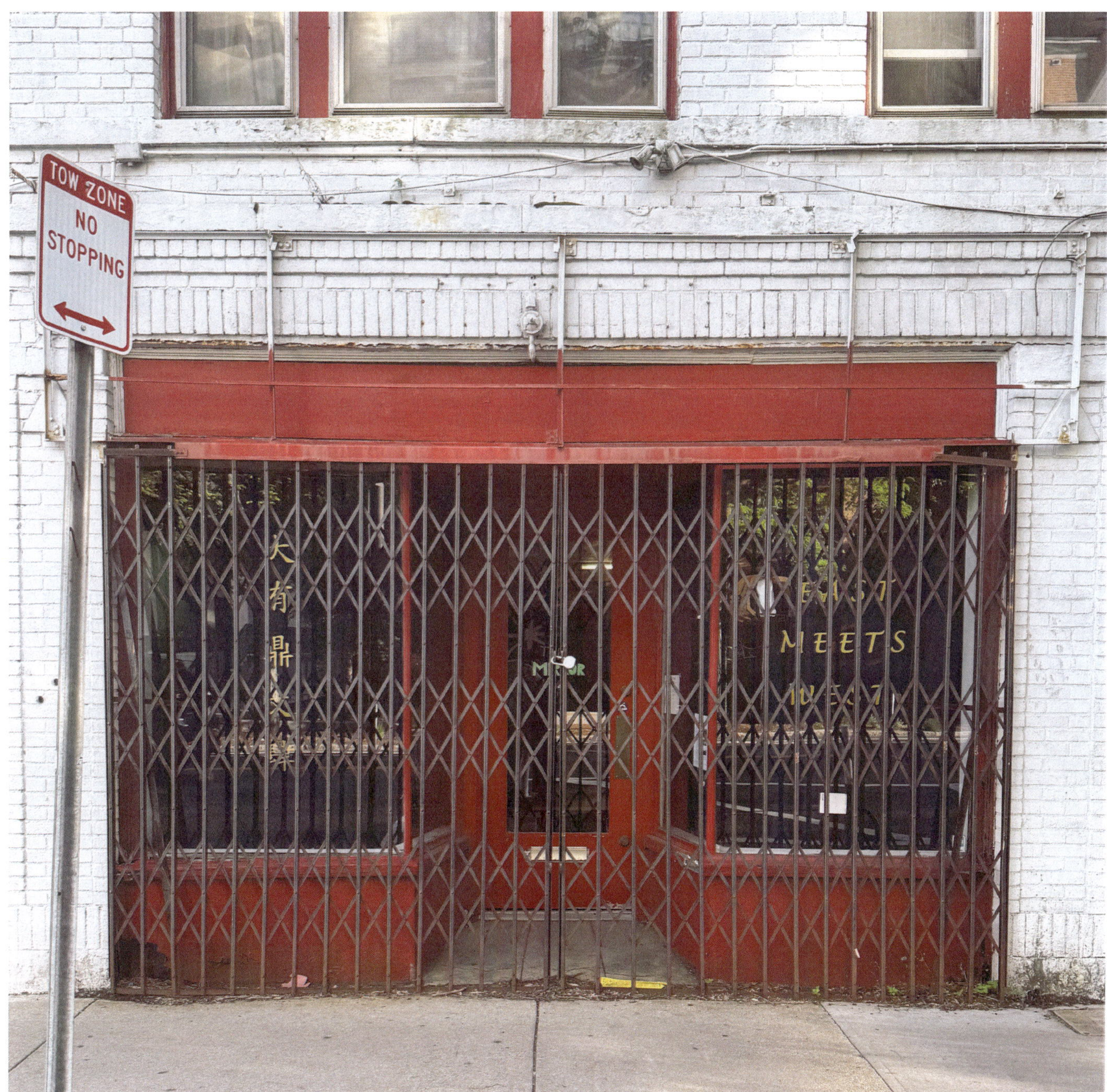
TOW ZONE
NO STOPPING
大有鼎文樂
EAST
MEETS
WEST

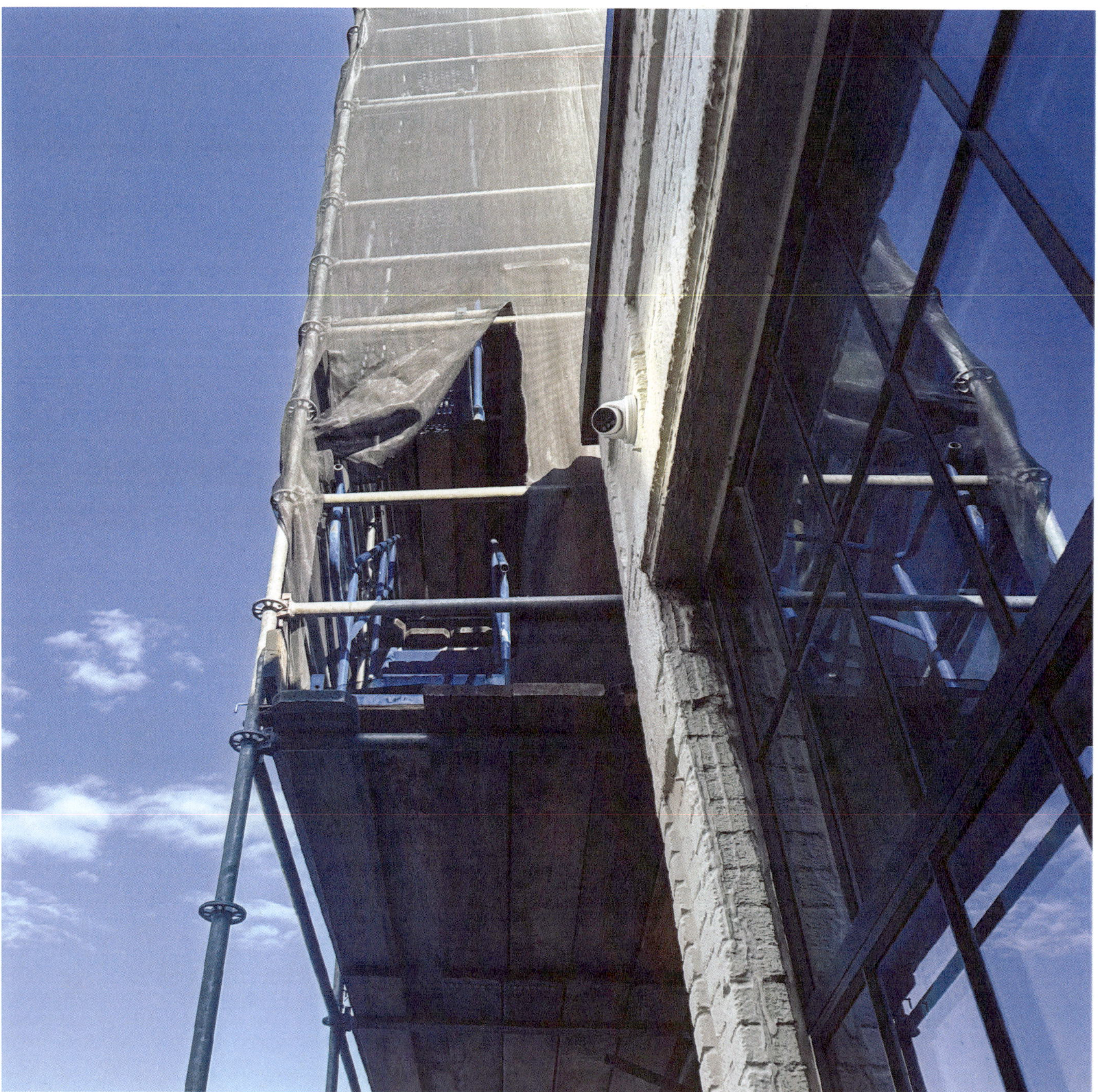

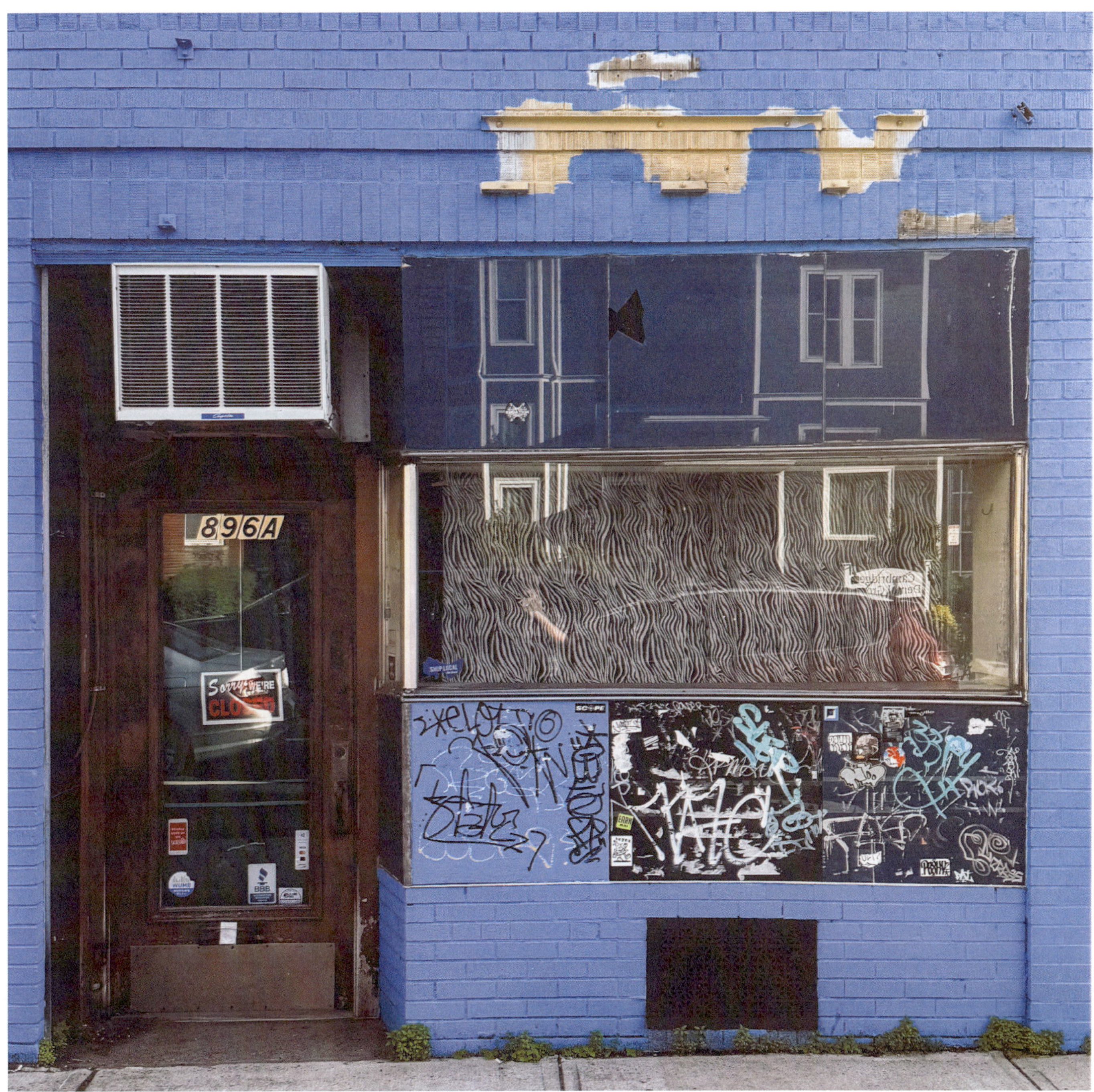
896A
Sorry WE'RE CLOSED

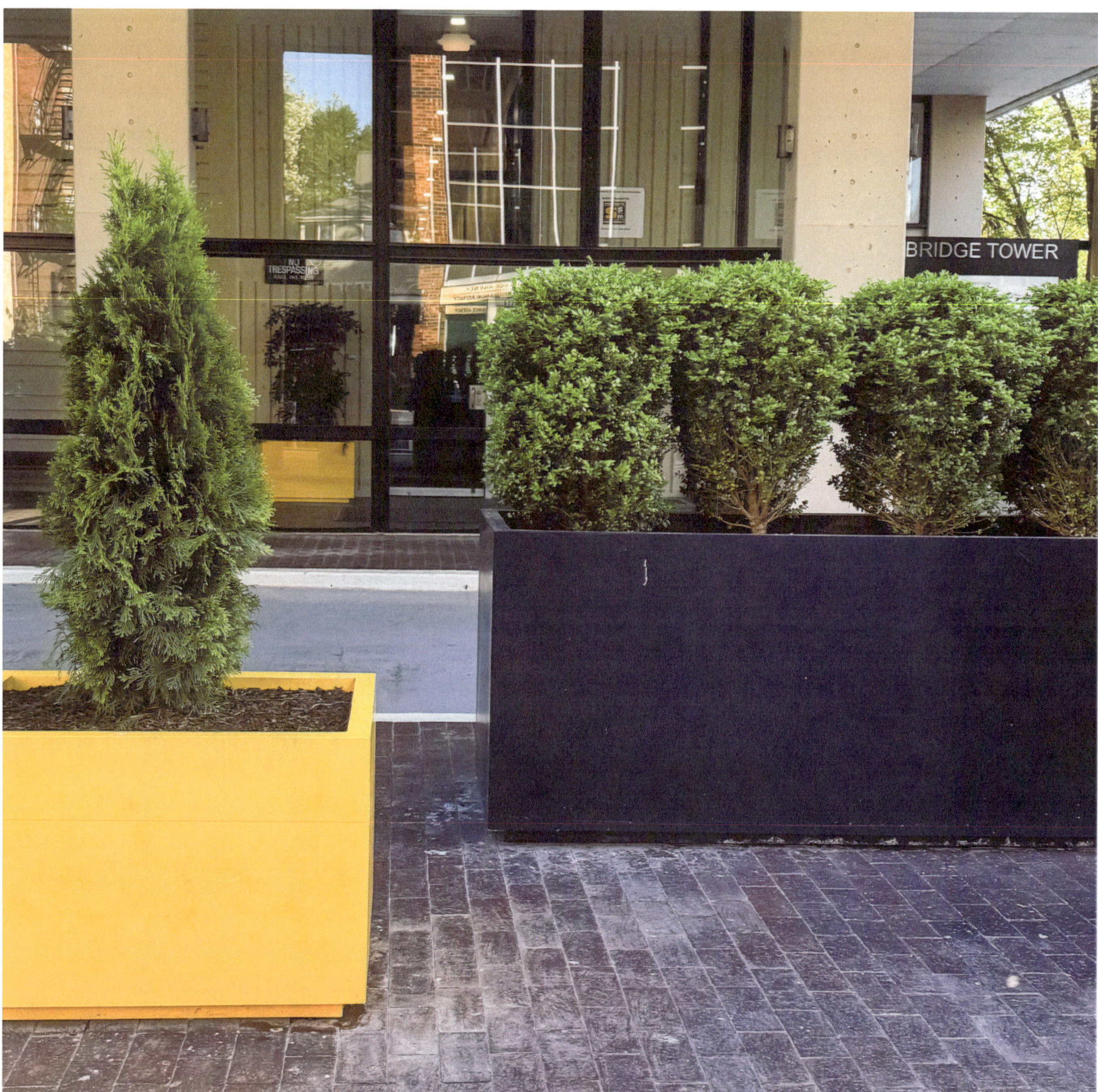
BRIDGE TOWER

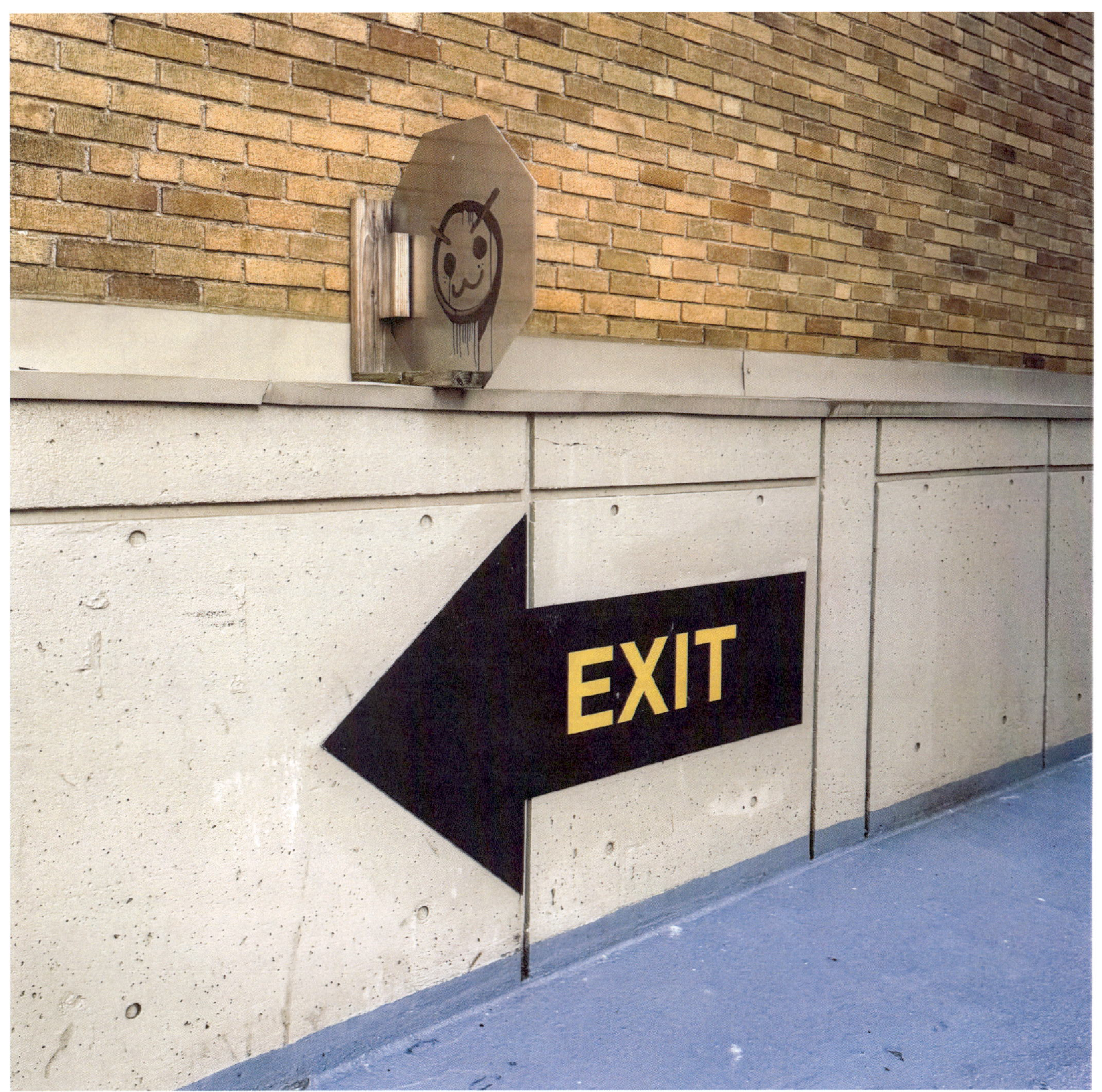
EXIT

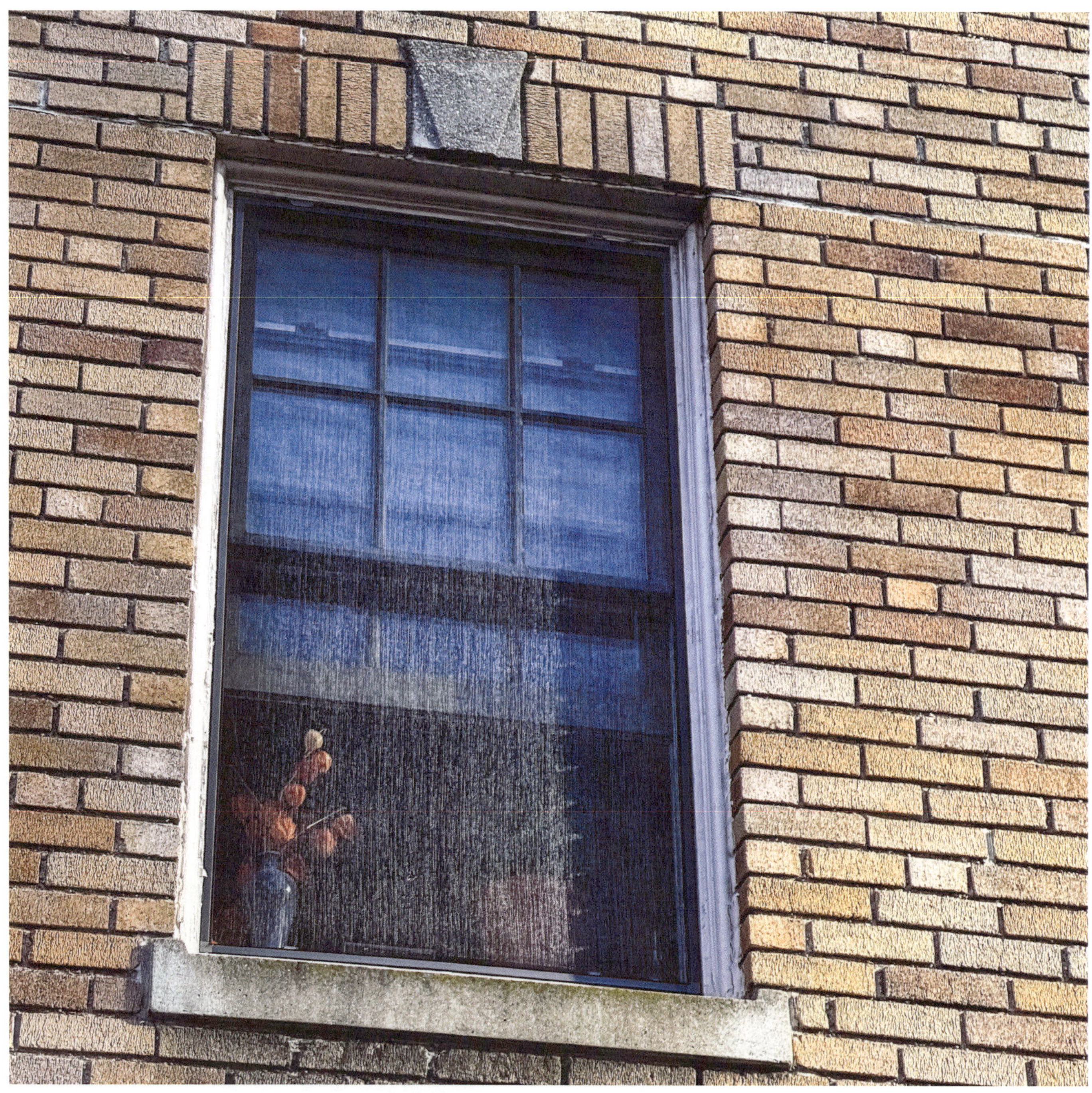

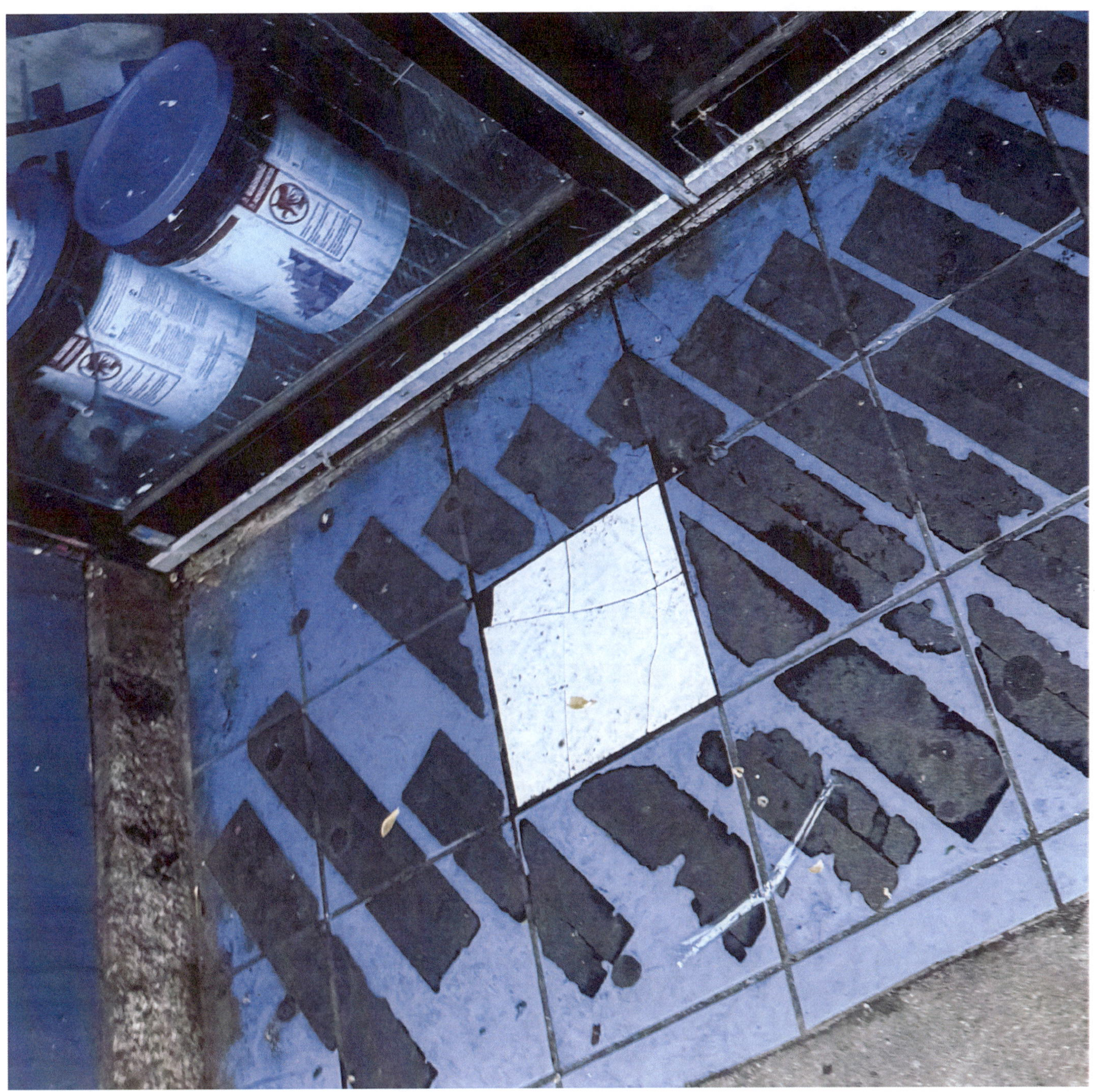

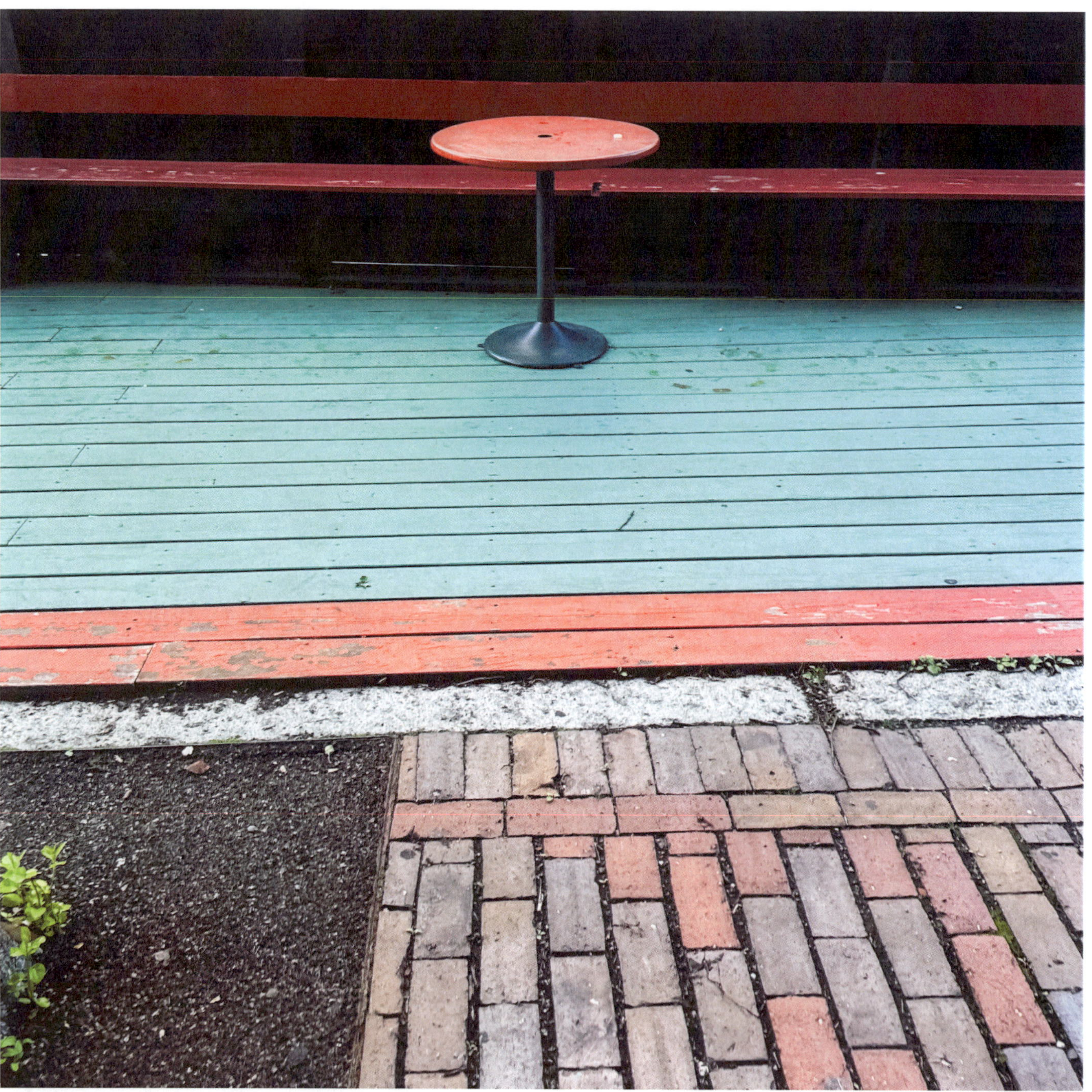

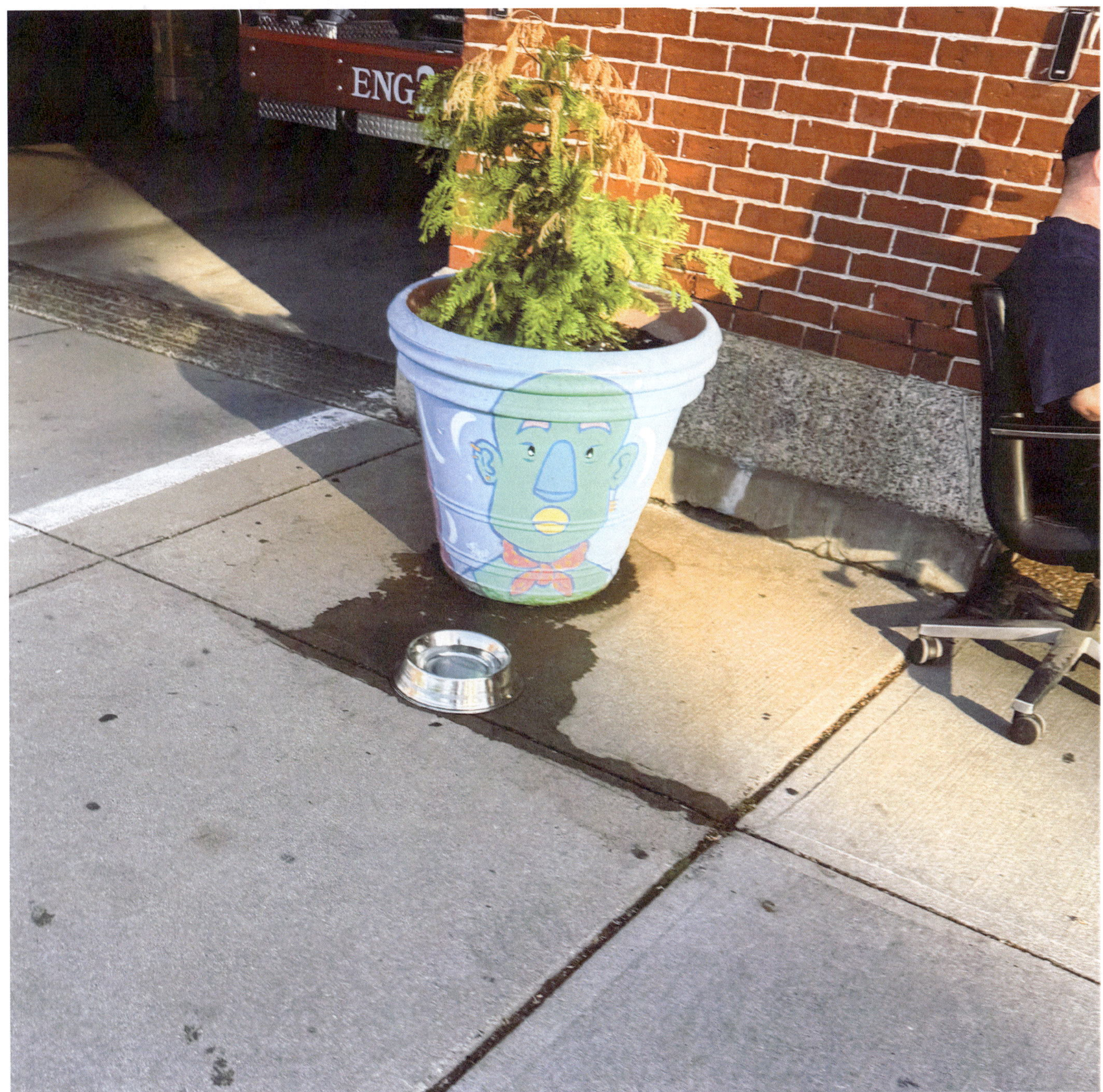
ENG

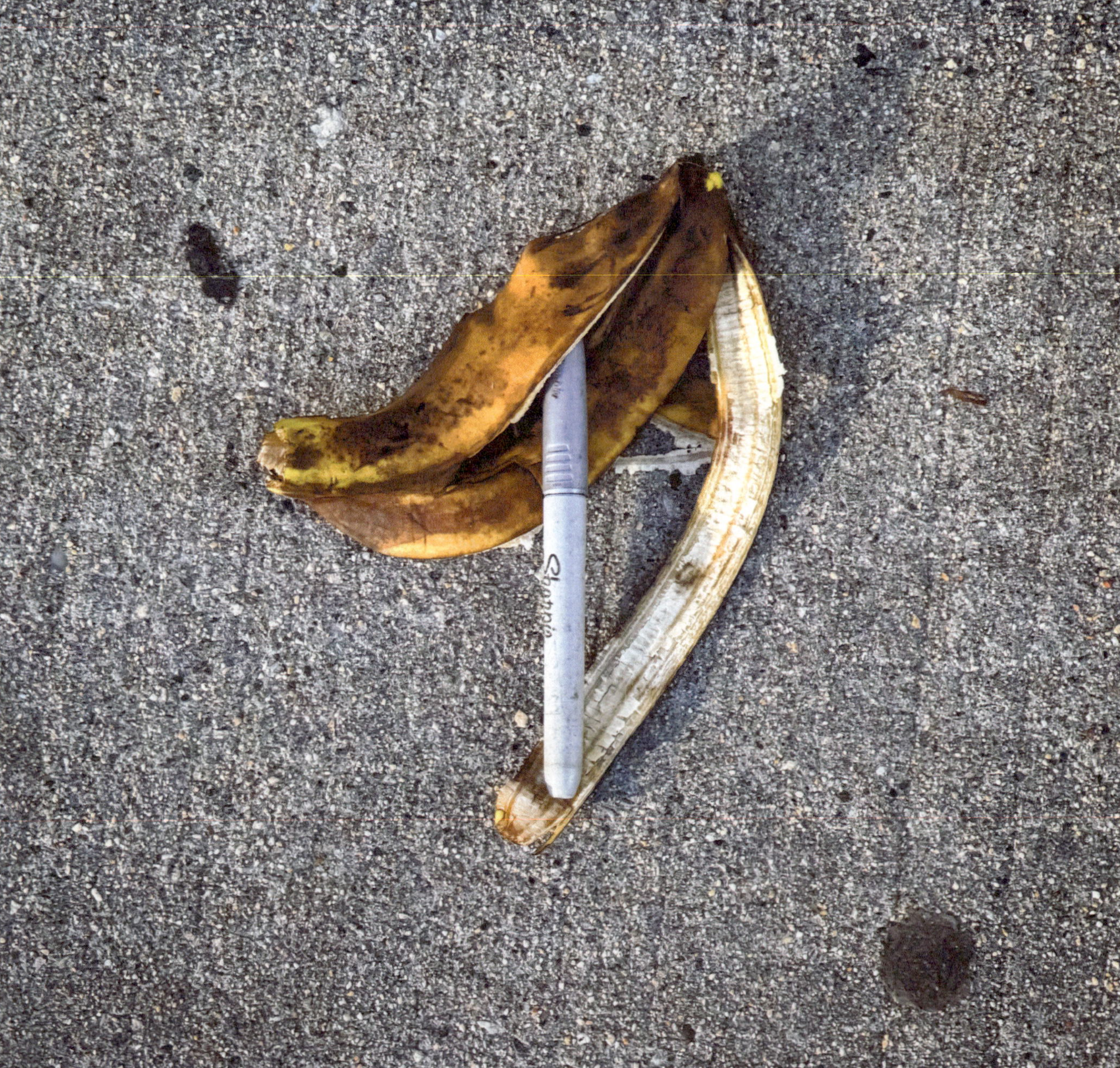

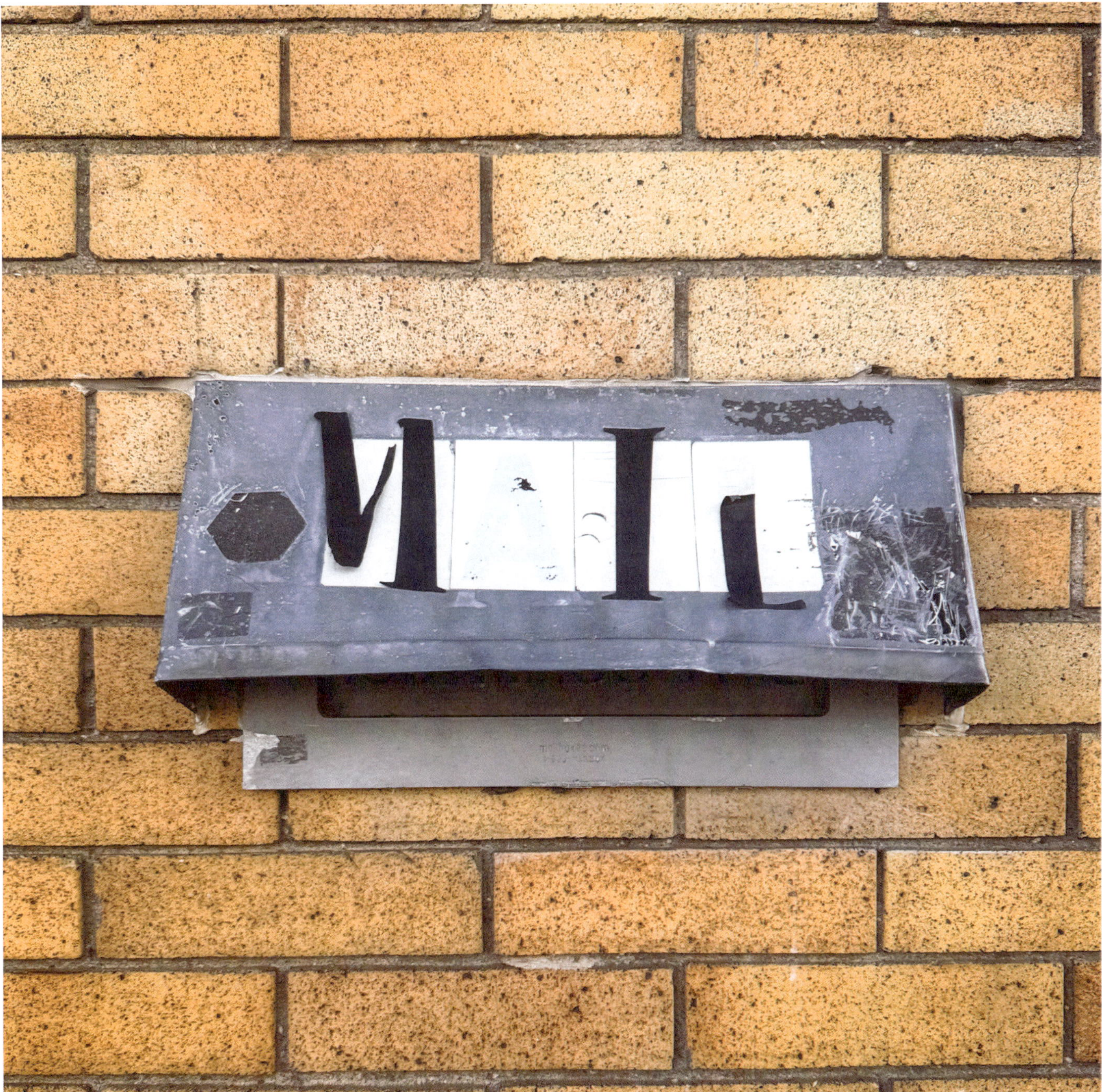

MAIN

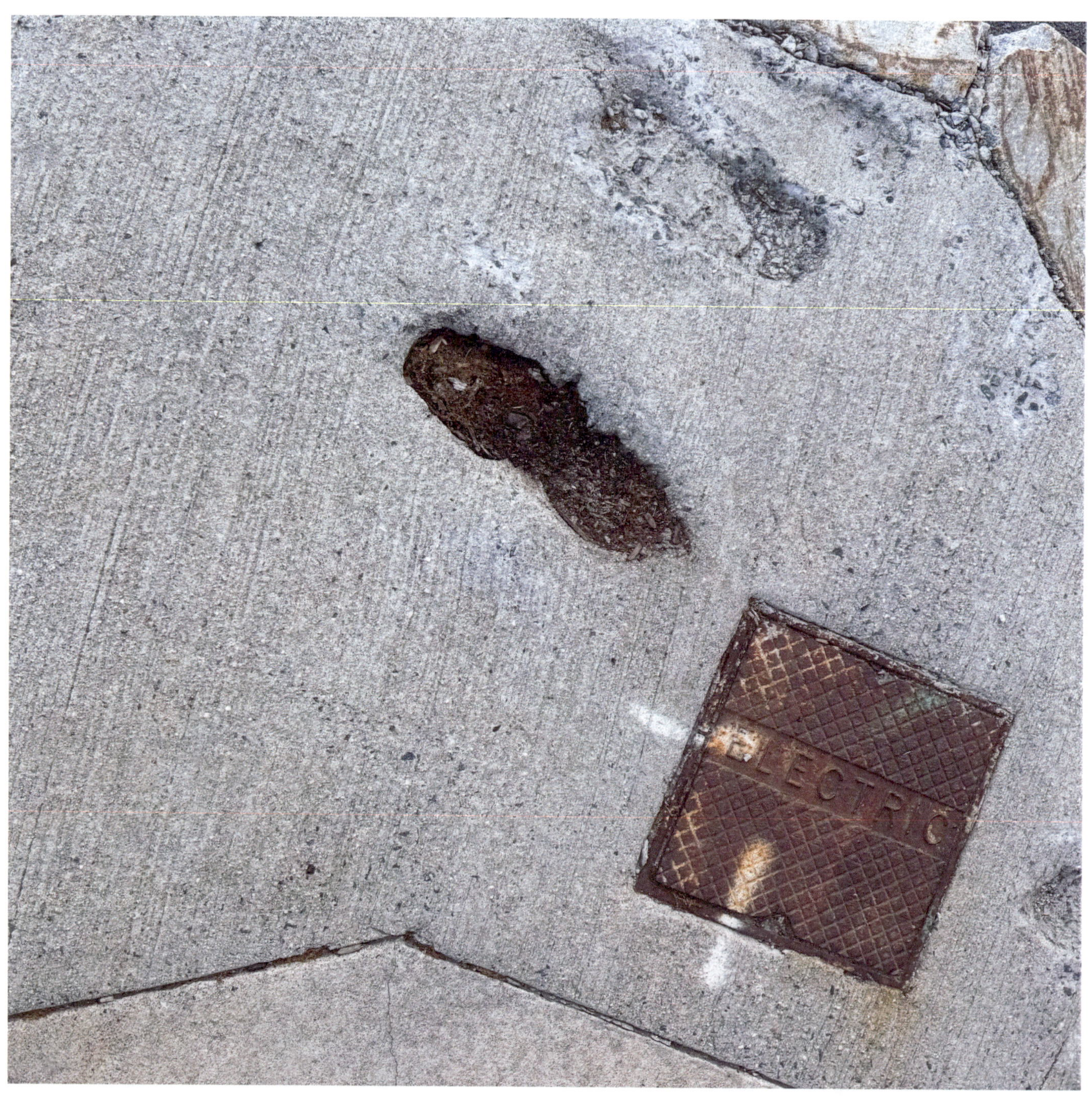

ELECTRIC

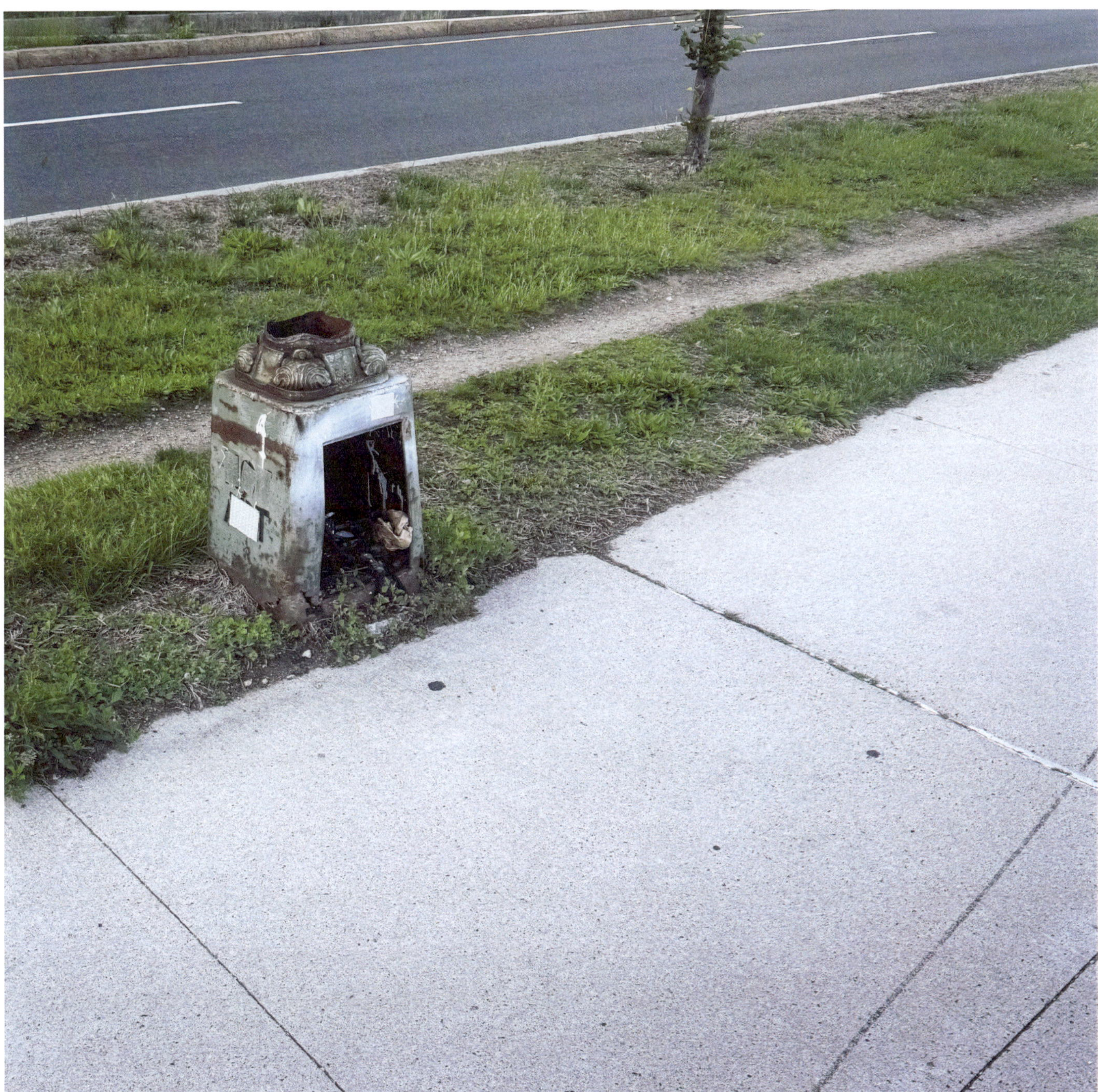

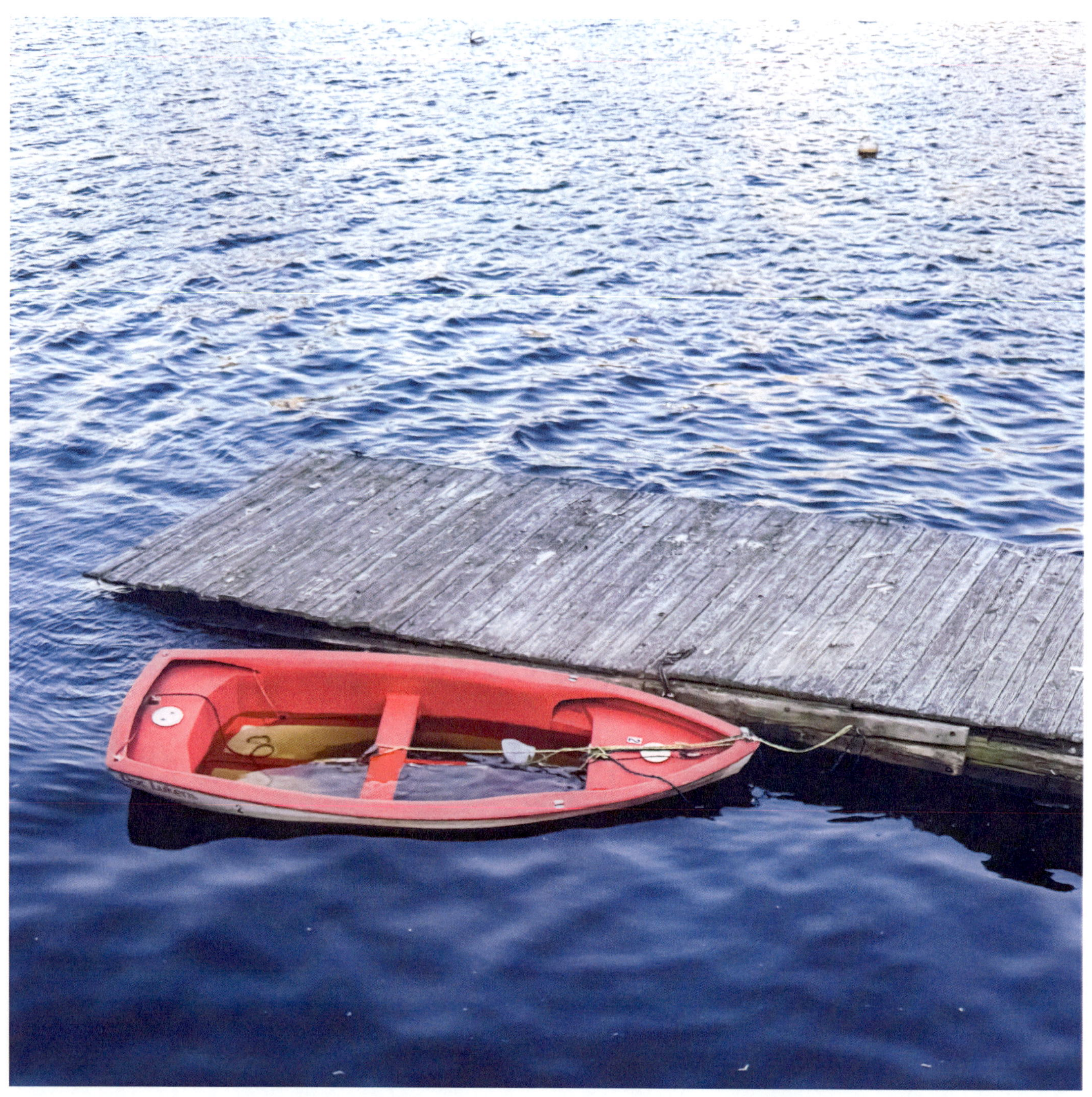

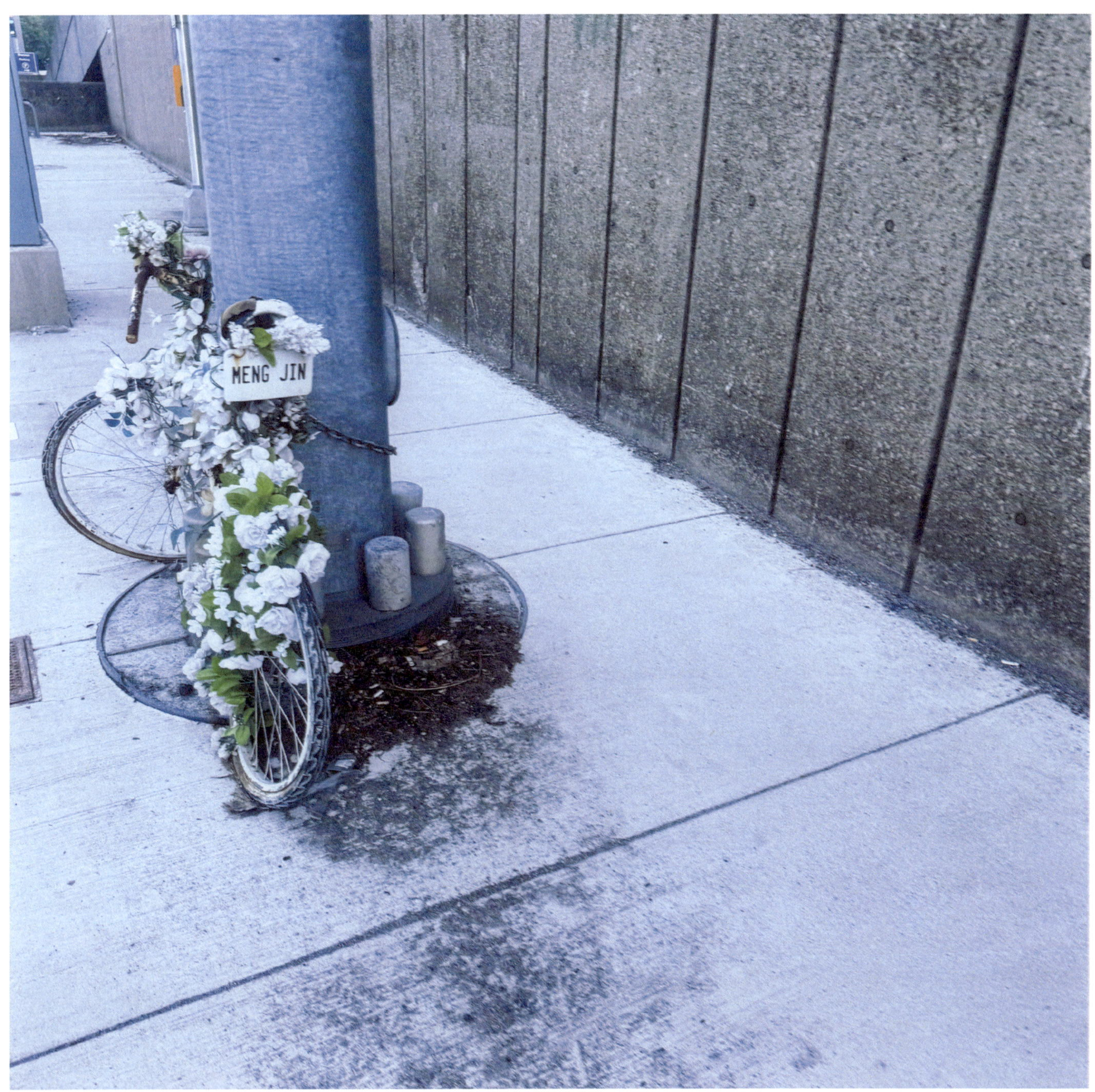

MENG JIN

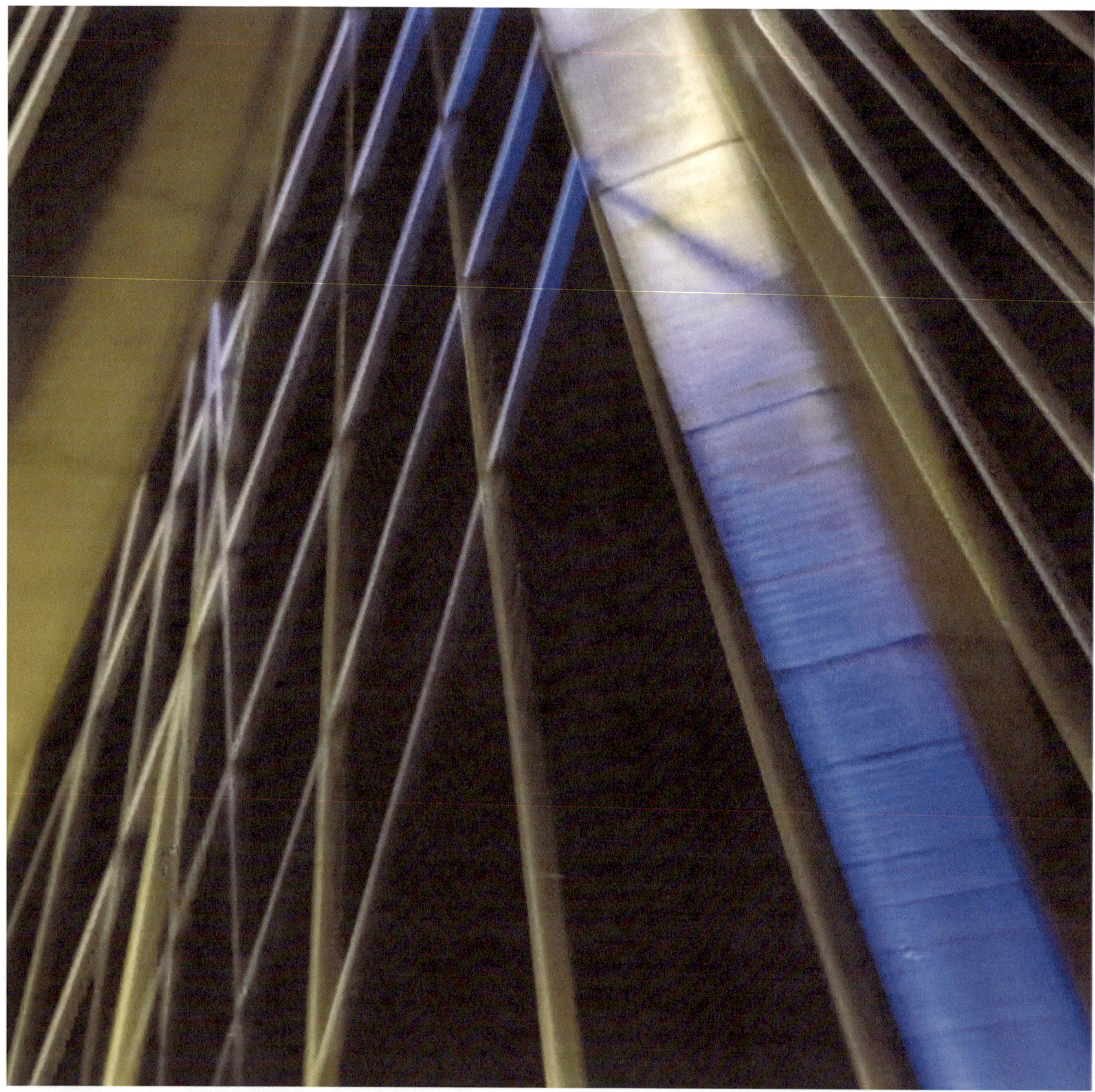